IT WAS MURDER!

IT WAS MURDER!

FORMER CHIEF SUPERINTENDENT
JOHN COURTNEY

BLACKWATER PRESS

Editor
Susannah Gee

Consultant Editors
Tim Ryan and John Garvey

Design & Layout
Susannah Gee

ISBN
0 86121 668 7

© 1996 John Courtney
British Library Cataloguing-in-Publication Data.
A catalogue record for this book is available from The British Library.
Courtney, John It Was Murder!

Produced in Ireland by
Blackwater Press,
c/o Folens Publishers,
8 Broomhill Business Park,
Tallaght,
Dublin 24

Printed in Ireland at the press of the Publisher.

ACKNOWLEDGEMENTS

I would like to convey my thanks to my son John, my daughter Breda, Supreme Court Judge Hugh O'Flaherty, and Tom McCaughran of RTE for their invaluable assistance. Without them this book would never have come to fruition.

The publishers would like to thank the following for permission to reproduce photographs: Garda Headquarters (Phoenix Park, Dublin), *The Irish Times*, Photocall.

Cover photographs supplied by: Garda Headquarters, *The Irish Times*.

CONTENTS

FOREWORD

When John Courtney first joined the Garda Síochana in 1947 there was little crime in Ireland. A change was noticeable in the 1960s and things began to turn really serious with the murder of Garda Richard Fallon in 1970. Patrick McLaughlin (afterwards Commissioner McLaughlin) revitalised the Murder Squad during his tenure there from 1961 to 1967. He recruited the best and brightest to that squad and he brought standards of expertise and efficiency to rival any force in the world. I was impressed with an example of the high ethical standards that he brought to his work in the first murder case that I was involved in as a young barrister in 1961.

Among those recruited by Patrick McLaughlin was John Courtney, then a young station sergeant at Clondalkin, Co. Dublin.

How inspired that choice was will be gleaned from the episodes set forth in this book. All human life is represented — from the sordid to the gallant — but we learn that good police work involves a great deal of hard slogging with little glamour.

The Garda Síochana occupy a special place in Irish life and culture as well as in the affection of the people. The force, like our language, is part of what we are.

John Courtney was moulded in the best tradition of the force: painstaking, courteous, but also wise in the ways of the world and the foibles of human nature.

This collection provides a commentary on how this society of ours has drifted into crime, where human life has proved all too dispensable. Yet as long as the job of keeping the peace is in as good hands as those of the same ilk as John Courtney, we have a measure of consolation and reassurance. John, of course, has not devoted himself exclusively to a life of beating crime — he was a formidable Kerry footballer in his day and is a loyal member of the Kerry Association in Dublin.

I wholeheartedly recommend this book of true detective stories to one and all.

Mr Justice Hugh O'Flaherty

The Supreme Court

Four Courts

Dublin

September 1996

INTRODUCTION

DÁ FHAD é an Lá, tagann an oíche (However long the day, night always comes). The wisdom of this seanfhocal applies to us all. After more than 43 years' service in the Garda Síochana, I finally hung up my uniform in 1991 and returned to being a private citizen.

I enjoyed my life as a member of the Gardaí, at all ranks up to Chief Superintendent, even though I had some very stressful moments. It was a world very far removed from the one I knew as a young boy growing up in Annascaul in Kerry, a county that has contributed many personnel to the Garda Síochana. Among them was Muiris O'Suilleabháin, who later wrote a book on life on the Blasket Islands which was translated into many languages.

I joined in the Spring of 1947 when I was 19, at the invitation of Sergeant Thomas Walshe in my native Annascaul. At the time I was working in my aunt's, Mrs Hannah Devane, store, unloading cement which I would draw by pony and cart from Annascaul Railway Station. I went into the garda station and completed the required forms. I was surprised that the sergeant had asked me to join as I often felt afterwards that he thought I was too republican in my views.

I did the examination and was called to training in Templemore in November, 1947.

I enjoyed my new career but greatly missed home, especially playing football with Dingle in the Kerry County Championship and with the Kerry Minors. I also missed the beauty of Kerry and chatting with the local people, including the many local characters. I knew practically everyone between Annascaul and Dingle from cycling every day to

Dingle CBS. Local contacts proved invaluable in my Garda career and I always made a point of developing them. Good police work is based on local knowledge and on winning the confidence of people.

My first posting was to Cork city. It was not my first visit, as I had played there with the Kerry Minors the previous year, when we won the Munster Final. I had been left with some reservations about the Cork people after that game! But as I got to know them, I found them most hospitable and helpful. Years later I was given their full co-operation when I went there to investigate the murder of a young girl, Colette Cronin, in Togher.

My switch to the Murder Squad came about from my work in Clondalkin, Co. Dublin, which was a difficult area to police in the early 1960s. There I helped in the investigation of many serious crimes and my work was recognised by Detective Superintendent Patrick McLaughlin — later Garda Commissioner — who transferred me to the Serious Crime Squad, or Murder Squad, of which he had charge.

The Murder Squad was a small and élite group of gardaí, which grew in strength in response to the rapid increase in serious crime in the early 1970s, following the outbreak of Northern troubles. The Murder Squad was formed in 1934, with a limited number of men and was still a relatively small unit when I joined it in 1967. But as the level of crime increased, so too, did the size of the Squad. At its peak it had some 30 members.

Much of the work involved preparing reports and assessing statements. The unit was based at Garda Headquarters in the Phoenix Park, but we moved around the country when investigating. We would set up an office in the area of the crime, with at least five men permanently based there. One officer logged all reports from the public and was responsible for investigating them. Another read and cross-checked statements and put the evidence together. A third officer prepared questionnaires which were completed by Gardaí during house-to-house inquiries, for all people over 10 years old living in the area where the crime was committed. The members of the public were asked to account for their whereabouts at the time that the crime was committed and to include any observations they made. The assistance gleaned from these forms often proved to be invaluable to our investigations. Inaccuracies in people's accounts were often found when they were cross-checked, giving vital clues. Yet another officer, usually a detective sergeant, was in charge of suspects while another member was in charge of searches. The objective was to co-ordinate all aspects of the investigation.

The murder of Garda Richard Fallon in the early 1970s, following a Dublin bank raid, marked the start of a major escalation in crime for which neither the Government nor the Gardaí were prepared. The violence in the North spread quickly across the Border, with bank robberies, murders and shootings of all kinds. I was put in charge of many of the investigations.

One of my toughest tasks was to ensure the various units worked together — the Technical Bureau, the Central Detective Unit (CDU), the Special Detective Unit (SDU) and the District Detective Unit (DDU). They were all separate units, but from time to time I found it necessary to remind them that they were all part of one Force, working for one objective — to combat subversive and serious crime. I managed to get that message across over time and members of the various units travelled all over the Republic with me, working together to solve various murders and other serious crimes.

The civilian personnel in the Garda stations around the country also played their part and I would like to pay tribute to them. While their duties were often simply to type reports, they would invariably offer expert advice and assistance which was much appreciated.

The establishment of the Forensic Science Laboratory in the early '70s, under Dr Jim Donovan, was also of immense value to the Murder Squad. Their painstaking work of piecing together evidence was often crucial to our investigations — so much so, in fact, that Dr Donovan was singled out for attack by criminal elements. Thankfully he survived to continue his excellent work.

Giving evidence in court was a major part of our work and we had to learn the law and how to present a case properly. During the years I got to know many of the leading prosecuting counsel, who are now very senior members of the judiciary. These include the President of the Supreme Court, Liam Hamilton, and Supreme Court Judge, Hugh O'Flaherty. Liam Hamilton taught me a lot about the criminal law and how to investigate cases. I learned from him precisely the type of information he would need, and I was always grateful to him for his help.

I also had great admiration for Judge O'Flaherty, who prosecuted many major cases for the State. He taught me a lot about the presentation of a case, down to the need for a detailed timetable of the prisoner's movements while in custody. He also instructed me on the proper layout of exhibition charts.

On the other side, defending prisoners, we had leading counsel such as Seamus Sorohan and Patrick McEntee. I always tried to impress on gardaí to have their homework well done and their evidence carefully prepared before they went to court.

I remember one cross-examination in particular. I was giving evidence at the trial following the murder of Senator Billy Fox. Seamus Sorohan, defending, asked me if I was excited when I had managed to secure a critical statement. I said I was not.

'Would you ever be excited?' he asked.

'Maybe, on some occasions,' I volunteered.

'Would you be excited if Kerry scored a goal in an All-Ireland Final?' he asked.

'Indeed, I would not, because that's a fairly common occurrence!' I replied.

Even the judge joined in the laughter. It was the first time Kerry had scored in the Special Criminal Court.

While we were on different sides of the fence, we had a great respect for each other. I particularly admired Sorohan and McEntee and also Martin Kennedy, now deceased.

I often spent days in the witness box being cross-examined and under a fair bit of pressure. Many gardaí are often hurt and angered by the nature of cross-examination. But that is the way the system operates. I have known some excellent gardaí, who were first class at their job, but were very afraid of the witness box. I always advised them to be prepared and to tell the truth. If you do that, there is nothing to worry about.

I also admired Garett Cooney, another leading counsel, and his brother, Paddy Cooney, who was probably the best Minister for Justice in my time. I would rank Gerry Collins next to him as a man who put everything into the job. Paddy Cooney always made a point of visiting the family when a Garda member was murdered, and was very supportive in general.

He had an advantage in being a solicitor. I have always believed that whoever is appointed Minister for Justice should have legal training, either as a barrister or a solicitor, and have a thorough understanding of the law. That, in my view, is absolutely essential.

Taking all serious crime into account, we had during those years a success rate of over 90 per cent, which was higher than any other police force in the world. That was not due to me, but to all the units of the Force, who worked together as a team.

I would also like to pay tribute to the uniformed personnel, who played a key role in crime investigation. In many cases, the public prefer to offer information to a uniformed garda than to a plain clothes detective. A case in point was the Herrema kidnapping. One of the Ferenka employees, who was associated with the Provisional IRA, felt duty bound to offer information to the Garda out of respect for his boss. But he didn't approach the detectives leading the investigation. Instead, he went to a Limerick Garda station and spoke to a uniformed officer.

Apart from investigating serious crime, which took up most of my time, I gave lectures for members of the Force, who had been promoted, on police work and on how to present evidence in court. We also gave courses to members of the Army, from Corporal to Commandant.

Over those 20 years I visited almost every town in the Republic in our efforts to solve crimes of all kinds. Many of the cases made news headlines and we were constantly under the media spotlight. Some of the cases, like the murder of Nurse Bridie Gargan in the Phoenix Park by Malcolm McArthur — which led to the coining of the phrase GUBU — and the blowing up of Lord Mountbatten, still arouse intense interest.

Apart from murders, we had to deal with kidnappings, a new phenomenon of which we had no experience. The kidnappings of Dr Tiede Herrema and Don Tidey were significant markers in the recent history of serious crime on this island. Both were successfully resolved, thanks to the co-operation of members of the Gardaí, but in the Tidey case, two members of the security forces paid with their lives.

Despite such sacrifices, we had our detractors. Allegations about a so-called 'Heavy Gang' hurt me very much, given the amount of effort which I and my colleagues had put into combatting crime and helping to preserve the security of the State, often at risk to our lives. I question the motives of those who spread the 'Heavy Gang' rumours.

Finally, I would like to pay tribute to all the colleagues who helped me over the years, and without whose co-operation I would not have been able to do my job, especially the late Dan Murphy who was a great colleague and advisor. A word of thanks must also go to the members of the Murder Squad. They have all served their country well and can be justly proud of their achievements. I would also like to thank the members of the general public for their constant help and co-operation in the on-going fight against crime. Without their continued support, the Garda Síochana cannot hope to win this battle.

It is all too often forgotten that members of the Gardaí are family men too, with wives and children who have to cope with the irregular hours and long absences from home, which the work entails. That calls for tolerance, understanding and support from the whole family if the officer — and the Force — are to function effectively.

My wife Mary and my five children gave me that support in full measure in what must often have been very trying circumstances for them. I would like publicly to acknowledge my debt to them and to say 'Thank You'.

1　THE DEADLY REVENGE OF A PIMP...

IT WAS one of the most obscene murder cases with which I ever had to deal with it. Revenge was the motive and three women died, slowly, painfully, and horribly in an arson attack on their home.

This was the Dublin netherworld of pimps and prostitution, of sex and savagery, where one woman had the courage to make a stand against the viciousness of an evil and dangerous man. Dolores Lynch, just 34, paid for her bravery with her life, dying in agony in a Dublin hospital with 70 per cent of her body covered in burns.

The revenge attack also cost the lives of her mother, Kathleen, aged 61, and her 67-year-old aunt, Hannah Hearne. But the man responsible for this triple horror was unrepentant. When he heard that Dolores Lynch had died, he told a woman friend: 'I'm glad. Anybody that rats deserves to be dead.'

It was early on Sunday, 16 January 1983 that the fire started downstairs at No. 15 Hammond Street, Blackpitts, off Clanbrassil Street in Dublin, quickly engulfing the house.

Dolores Lynch was asleep in the rear upstairs bedroom while her mother and aunt shared an upstairs front bedroom. Neighbours tried to rescue them. Two men eventually climbed up to the second floor and found Dolores trying to get out of a small window, with the flames closing in on her. After a desperate struggle, they managed to pull the badly burnt woman to safety.

Nothing could be done for Hannah and Kathleen. Dolores Lynch was taken to the Casualty Department of St James's Hospital with extensive first and second degree burns covering about 70 per cent of her body.

She was conscious and asked a nurse how her mother was. The medical staff did not tell her that her mother was dead. She said: 'No one is telling me, but I know my mother and aunt must be dead because they did not come into the hospital with me.' She was anointed by a priest before being transferred to Dr Steven's Hospital.

Her uncle and aunt visited her. Dolores recognised them and said: 'Uncle Jim, my mammy is dead.' She repeated this over and over. He told her that he was going to visit her mother and Aunt Hannah in St James's Hospital, but Dolores replied: 'She is not in St James's Hospital, She is dead, dead, dead.' Some hours later Dolores herself died from her dreadful injuries.

The Murder Squad was called in as there had been a previous attempt to set fire to the house. Firelighters were pushed through the letter-box and the hallway set alight. A search of the back yard revealed three small boxes of matches and a cigarette lighter. Inside the house, underneath the debris of the first or second step of the stairs, was a single block of a white firelighter. Beside it were two pieces of coal and a shrivelled piece of blue material.

Dolores's uncle told us that he had foiled the previous arson attempt in April 1982. On his way home from a card game at 2.30 a.m., he had discovered a fire in the hallway. He extinguished the firelighters and wakened the women. Then he reported the incident to the Gardaí.

Meanwhile, in a cruel footnote to the tragedy, someone had painted 'Dolores Lynch is a rat' on a wall at St James's Hospital. The message was written in silver paint and a sample of it was taken for forensic examination. It offered our first clue to the killer's identity. It was now clear that Dolores was the intended victim and that her mother and aunt had died because they happened to be in the house at the time. So who was Dolores Lynch, and why should someone want to kill her?

She was born on 10 February 1948, the second eldest of four daughters. She left school at 14 and worked with her mother in a factory in Dublin, before becoming a chambermaid in the Montrose Hotel.

Her father, we discovered, had had an incestuous affair with her and a child was stillborn. After that she left home and became a prostitute. She

THE DEADLY REVENGE OF A PIMP…

had 20 criminal convictions, dating from 1966 to 1979, for prostitution, housebreaking and larceny.

However, in 1980 she quit the life of a prostitute and was employed as a wardsmaid in St James's Hospital, a job she kept until her death. We discovered it was something which happened while she was still working as a prostitute that created the grudge which led to the murder and those of her mother and aunt. Three informants supplied us with the details and the name of the killer. Dolores had made a statement to the Gardaí at Donnybrook some years earlier about an assault on her. It read:

At 11.45 p.m. on 11 May 1976 I was in the company of Catherine, Alice and Marian in the Kentucky Fried Chicken Restaurant at Upper Baggot Street. We were having chips and sitting at the seats near the windows when John Cullen came in. John Cullen walked up to us and asked us if there was a cigarette machine on the premises. Somebody said it was up at the counter.

He walked up to the counter and asked for some cigarettes and a bottle of coke. He was told by the man serving that they did not have bottles, only cans of coke. He bought a can of 7-Up. A friend of John Cullen's then walked to the front door and put his foot and arm against the door, which was completely closed.

John Cullen then walked over to us. He turned to me and without warning hit me on the head with the can of 7-Up. He then asked me if I knew him. I did not answer him and he hit me again with the can of 7-Up. I then said that I did not know him, or that I did not want to know him. He kicked me in the stomach and I doubled up.

He kicked me in the eye and chest. He continued to hit me on the head with the can until he drew blood. He also turned me around to face his friend and said: 'If you know him on Friday, you will get it.' His friend said: 'you will be dead'.

He kicked me and hit me several more times. Before he left he said that if I go to Court on Friday to give evidence, in a case pending against him, that I would be killed stone dead. Then they left and remained outside for 20 minutes. We had to stay until some customers came into the restaurant before we could get out of the place, as we were scared to leave.

9

I was taken to St Vincent's Hospital, where I received 10 stitches in two wounds in my head. My right eye was badly injured and was closed for five days. I was detained in hospital but was allowed to leave the following day.

Dolores had told the Gardaí about the attack and as a result of the ensuing court case, John Cullen was found guilty and spent three years in jail. Dolores had been brave to stand up to a vicious, dangerous man, but he never forgot or forgave what she had done and swore he would kill her for 'squealing' on him.

On the 26 January 1983, 10 days after the murders, we interviewed a former friend of Dolores, a woman named Grace. She told us that the day after the fire, Elizabeth, a prostitute who worked for John Cullen, called to her flat in Ballymun.

Elizabeth said to me that her nerves were gone, and I told her that Dolores Lynch, whom we both know, was dead. Elizabeth just nodded her head, signifying that's why her nerves were gone. At this stage, John Cullen was in the sitting room watching television and Elizabeth went into the room to tell him that Dolores Lynch was dead. I heard him reply that he was glad, and that now she would not be able to rat any more. My boyfriend came in and he and John Cullen watched television and Elizabeth and I went into the bedroom. Then she told me what happened at Hammond Street on the Sunday morning.

Elizabeth said that John Cullen and herself went to Dolores Lynch's house in Hammond Street, in his car. He brought two containers of petrol, which she said he had had for about a year. When they got there, he went to have a look at the house. He said there was a light on. Then he went back in with the petrol.

She waited outside because she could not climb the wall. He put the petrol in the downstairs, at the back. He did not even have to break in because the window was open. She could see his head through the window as it was lighting. John Cullen had told her to watch the windows on either side. Elizabeth told me that this happened sometime around 4 a.m. She did not want to go to Hammond Street but that she was afraid that John Cullen might harm her if she did not go.

Before they left Hammond Street, Elizabeth said she heard Dolores Lynch screaming: 'get me mother out'. She wanted to go back in to help Dolores but John Cullen pulled her away. They went back to his car and drove back to Elizabeth's flat in Ballymun. On the way back to the flat John Cullen said to Elizabeth, who was panicking: 'It's alright, they'll get out.' Later he said: 'I hope it is the right house'.

Elizabeth told Grace that when they arrived at the flat, Cullen said he was glad he had done it. She also said they had got rid of all the clothes they were wearing that night. They drove somewhere far into the hills, where there was water. They tore up their clothes, bit by bit, including her black fur jacket, and disposed of them in pieces. She was scared stiff that John Cullen was going to throw her off the cliff. Grace also told us that she met John Cullen at 2 a.m. on Saturday, 22 January, in Dublin's Herbert Street.

He brought me to my flat in Ballymun in his red Datsun car. On the way, he asked me who had made the collection for Dolores Lynch and he said that they had an awful cheek making a collection for her. He said he was glad she was dead and he wanted to know if she died screaming. He said: 'I hope the maggots are eating her'. He was clenching the steering wheel with both hands and seemed to be in a rage. He said: 'She deprived me of my children for three years'. He was in my flat for about three hours altogether. He remarked several times, 'I am glad she is dead. She deserves to be dead. Anybody that rats deserves to be dead.'

Grace said he told her that if you wanted to get rid of somebody, you should burn them because that way you burn all the evidence as well. She also said he described how to start a fire outside a house by using a lighted cigarette, matches, firelighters and petrol.

He said he would probably be pulled in because Dolores Lynch had left statements with loads of people saying that if anything happened to her, he would be responsible. He said, 'I don't give a bollox, they will have to prove it. I don't let anybody away with anything. If someone does something on you, you get them back. It does not matter how you get them back. If someone hurts you, you hurt them back. Anything that anybody told the police about me, I'll get them back and I fucking got her back'. Then he realised what he said and he added, 'Well somebody got her back.'

Grace said she was forced to have sex with him 'because I was frightened of what he would do if I did not allow him. I did not report the matter to the Gardaí because I was afraid he would kill me if I did'.

Grace and Elizabeth shared a common background. Both had become prostitutes at 16. Elizabeth was born in Cork but when she was 7 years old her family broke up and she moved to England with her mother. She did not get along well with her mother and went to work on the streets. She lived with a man and had two children before returning to Dublin with him and having a third child. She later left her boyfriend and their three children and moved in with another man in Dublin.

Things did not work out, so she moved in with one of her sons in a flat in Ballymun. Her second boyfriend came to their flat one night and tried to break in. She got out of the flat by climbing a rope from the rear balcony, but slipped and broke her ankle. While she lay on the ground, her boyfriend stabbed her five times with a pair of scissors.

While in hospital she was visited by a number of friends including some prostitutes. This was how she met John Cullen. Her friend was a prostitute and Cullen was her pimp. One night he made a date with her and she began seeing him on a regular basis.

Her friend ran off with another man and Cullen told her she would have to become a prostitute to provide them with an income. She gave him all the money she earned on the streets.

She said that Cullen was always talking about Dolores Lynch, and was paranoid about her. He said he was going to kill her for getting him three years in prison and taking his kids away from him. She claimed he once told her that he had set fire to Dolores Lynch's flat but the fire went out. She told how on Saturday, 15 January, Cullen came to her flat and told her to get dressed. They went to Hammond Street, she told us, where he set fire to Dolores Lynch's house.

It was time to bring Cullen in, a man who was no stranger to Garda custody. He was born in 1950, in Drimnagh, in Dublin and left school at the age of 14. He was married with three children, two boys and a girl, but the family man image ended there. He was well known as a pimp and took 80 per cent of the prostitutes' earnings by using violence against them. He had 20 previous convictions against him, starting from when he was 10. They ranged from larceny to assault. At the time of his arrest for the murder of Dolores Lynch, he was already awaiting trial for assault.

Despite lengthy questioning, Cullen refused to make a written statement. But he agreed with the version of events given by Grace and Elizabeth. He insisted he had not intended to kill the three women and had believed they would escape from the blaze. Asked if he hated Dolores Lynch for having him jailed for three years, he replied: 'No, I felt she should not get away with it.'

John Cullen was found guilty of the murder of Dolores Lynch, and sentenced to penal servitude for life. At this time he is still in custody. After the trial, a relative commented that he had almost committed the perfect crime, disposing of all his clothes and other evidence that linked him to the fire. His one mistake, according to the relative, was taking along a woman who later revealed what he had done.

Thank heavens she did! For the horror perpetrated by John Cullen was typical of his viciousness. On one occasion during the trial he suddenly gave one of the prison wardens an unmerciful blow, for no reason. His lust for revenge against a defenceless woman, who had the courage to stand up to his violence, was such that it mattered little how many people died, so long as he succeeded in his warped ambition to get even. Three women's lives was a terrible price to pay for the injured ego of a brutal pimp.

2 MOUNTBATTEN KILLER ARRESTED BEFORE THE MURDER...

THE IRA man who murdered Lord Louis Mountbatten was actually in Garda custody when the bomb which killed him exploded. The suspicions of a patrol officer, on duty several miles from the murder scene, led to his arrest, and it added a bizarre dimension to the investigation.

However, in the Special Criminal Court, it was the results of a major painstaking operation by members of the Garda forensic team which connected the man to the murder and won a conviction. They were superb, and none more so than Dr Jim Donovan, head of the Forensic Section. It was his evidence, clear, precise and easily understood by the court, that helped put the killer behind bars. A year later he was to pay a high price for doing his duty in such an exemplary manner, when during another high-profile case a bomb exploded in his car, causing him serious leg injuries.

I was shocked by the attack on a highly-valued colleague, which happened, incidentally, as he drove past my home in Dublin. Dr Donovan was lucky to escape with his life, but the injuries left him in severe pain and distress for many years afterwards.

Lord Mountbatten had always been a prime target for the IRA, as a representative of the British Royalty. He was particularly close to the current heir to the British throne, Prince Charles, who regarded him as a favourite uncle and was reportedly shattered by his murder.

Every summer Lord Mountbatten, accompanied by family members and friends, travelled to his Irish holiday home, Classiebawn Castle in Mullaghmore, some eight miles from Sligo. He loved Mullaghmore and the locals were fond of their royal visitor.

Because of the IRA threat, he and his party were always given close Garda protection, but the tight security irritated him. He would not allow the Gardaí aboard his fishing boat, the Shadow V, which he kept in the local harbour, nor would he permit them to accompany him by speedboat when he went fishing.

Maybe the tranquillity of the small seaside village dulled the alertness of a man who was no stranger to security — he had been a British naval hero and a Viceroy of India. Maybe at 79, he just wanted a quiet life. Whatever the reason, his disregard for his personal safety was to prove fatal.

Mullaghmore was an unlikely setting for murder. The area is almost completely surrounded by water and only one road leads to the windswept, isolated village. Fishing boats bob up and down in the small, sheltered harbour between the houses and the sea. Tourists, mainly from Northern Ireland, descend on the area every summer, attracted by its sheer natural beauty.

From the sea, the land rises sharply upwards to a castle of grey cut stone. Like an ancient sentinel, Classiebawn Castle watches over Mullaghmore and Donegal Bay. That summer of 1979, Lord Mountbatten had arrived at Classiebawn in August. With him were his daughters, Lady Pamela and Lady Patricia, her husband Lord Brabourne, and their twin sons, Timothy and Nicholas. Other guests were the Dowager Lady Brabourne and a friend, Hugh Tunney.

Sailing was Lord Mountbatten's first passion, as might be expected with an old sea dog. His Shadow V fishing boat was 27 feet long, about ten years old and powered by a diesel engine. The boat was in far from mint condition, with its several layers of paint visibly peeling. Despite that, almost every day he would cruise out into the bay to fish or check his lobster pots.

On 27 August, the last day of his life, Lord Mountbatten and his family rose early. For breakfast he had two mackerel, his favourite fish. After kitting themselves out, they took the short drive to the harbour.

With Lord Mountbatten were his daughter, Lady Patricia, her husband and both their children Nicholas, and Timothy. There, too, were the Dowager Lady Brabourne and 15-year-old Paul Maxwell, the boat boy. They were in high spirits as they loaded the boat for the trip. Lord Brabourne took a last family photograph on the quayside before they set off slowly into the bay.

Keeping watch from the road on the cliff top were some gardaí. They had been instructed to keep their distance because of Lord Mountbatten's dislike of close security. They watched him steer the Shadow V through the calm waters towards the lobster beds.

Suddenly, to their horror, a massive explosion ripped through the boat, which disintegrated before their eyes. Bodies were flung into the sea and debris showered from the sky. The noise of the blast was heard miles away. The shocked gardaí rushed to the shore, the air now full of the agonised screams of survivors as they struggled in the water. Lord Mountbatten was dead. His legs had been shattered and he had drowned. Paul Maxwell, the boat boy, died instantly in the blast and his body was recovered from the water. Nicholas Brabourne was also dead, but his mother and father and brother Timothy had miraculously survived. The Dowager Lady Brabourne was seriously injured and rushed to Sligo Hospital. She died from her injuries the next day.

Lady Pamela, Lord Mountbatten's other daughter, had been lucky — she had decided not to go on the fishing trip that morning.

I travelled from Dublin with the Murder Squad to take charge of the investigation and talked first to Lady Pamela at Classiebawn Castle. Despite the very tragic circumstances she was totally in control and very cooperative. I was very impressed by her, given the fact that she was being interviewed by a policeman in what was to her a foreign country. Then I drove on to Sligo Hospital, where I interviewed Lord and Lady Brabourne. All three offered what help they could in the investigation.

The bomb appeared to have been set off by remote control, though a Garda search of the surrounding hills proved fruitless. The tragic irony is that the killer was already in custody, thanks to the vigilance of Garda J. Lohane, from Granard, Co. Longford, who was subsequently promoted. At 9.40 a.m. on 27 August, he stopped a car, four miles from Granard, to check its tax disc. He noticed the occupants were very nervous. The driver said his name was Patrick Rehill, but was unable to give the car's registration number. The passenger said he was Thomas McMahon and he, too, was visibly nervous. Neither man had any identification on him. Garda Lohane became so suspicious that the two were involved in some criminal activity that he called for assistance and the men were taken to Granard Garda Station for questioning.

Later that evening, after the Mullaghmore blast, a Garda recognised the man claiming to be Patrick Rehill as Francis McGirl, who was believed to be a republican sympathiser. Neither man would make a statement and both were arrested under Section 30 of the Offences Against the State Act, 1939.

Some time later, during questioning, Francis McGirl blurted out 'I put no bomb in the boat'.

'What boat?' asked a Garda.

'No answer,' replied Francis McGirl.

I was already aware that Thomas McMahon, a County Monaghan man, was an explosives expert and an active member of the Provisional IRA. We strongly suspected these two men of the murder blast, but one throwaway remark by Francis McGirl was not enough evidence to build a case on. Since, contrary to what a lot of people believed, we did not beat confessions from our suspects, we had to find the damning evidence somewhere else. We did so with the patience and help of a superb forensic team.

Firstly, we collected every piece of the fishing boat that we could find and then, like a huge jigsaw puzzle, we stuck the whole lot back together again. From this we discovered that the bomb had been placed near the engine. This meant that someone had to walk or swim to the boat, board it and get to the engine room. As I mentioned, the paintwork on the Shadow V was layered and flaking off. We took samples of this paint, from the outside of the vessel and some sand from the shore. Then we stripped the suspects' car and took all of their clothing, shoes and socks for analysis.

Sea shore sand varies from place to place. The sand on the shoes and socks of both Francis McGirl and Thomas McMahon was the same type as that in Mullaghmore, near the harbour. Green and white paint flakes from both the interior and exterior of the Shadow V were found on McMahon's shoes, clothing and on the car mat and seat on the passenger side of the car in which the two were travelling. Sea sand does not adhere to clothing for any long length of time, so we concluded they had been in Mullaghmore recently.

From studying the boat wreck we knew high explosives had been used. Traces of nitroglycerine and ammonium nitrate were found on the clothing of McMahon. At the height of the investigation I was contacted by a Chief Superintendent McCullagh from the RUC in the North. I travelled across the border to meet him but he had no information to offer on the case. He subsequently asked me if he could come down and view the scene but I said no. At the Special Criminal Court in Dublin, both men were charged with being members of the Provisional IRA and of the murder of Lord Mountbatten. They pleaded not guilty.

As I have said, Dr Jim Donovan, head of the Forensic Section, was one of the State's most important witnesses. He confirmed that nitroglycerine and ammonium nitrate were the main components of the gelignite, and that both substances had been found on McMahon's clothing. He gave evidence that the paint flakes and the sea sand discovered in the car and on McMahon's clothes, shoes and socks, matched the paint samples from the Shadow V and the sand from the shore in Mullaghmore. The odds against the paint flakes being different were 250,000 to 1. A micro-analyser machine was used to compare the sand samples by way of x-rays. They were identical. Other sand samples taken from other nearby beaches proved to be different. McGirl's clothing also contained samples of nitroglycerine and ammonium nitrate, and he had the same sand particles on his footwear as McMahon did.

The case for the prosecution rested heavily on forensic evidence. No one had seen either of them boarding the Mountbatten boat in the harbour, or being in the vicinity of Mullaghmore. In addition as the suspects were in custody miles away from Mullaghmore when the bomb exploded, it was obvious the evidence against them could only be forensic and circumstantial.

Dr Donovan put forward a very good case, one that convinced the Court despite being vigorously challenged by the men's defence team. The decisive evidence turned out to be the flakes of paint from the boat found on McMahon's clothing. The Court was satisfied that he handled the bomb and placed it on the Shadow V with the intention of killing those on board. He was found guilty of the murder of Lord Mountbatten and sentenced to life imprisonment. McMahon served his sentence in Portlaoise Prison and was one of a number of prisoners who were due for release on the day of the Canary Wharf bombing in London on 9 February 1996, when the releases were cancelled. McGirl was acquitted on lack of evidence and walked free from the Court. He recently died in a traffic accident.

Lord Mountbatten was given a state funeral in Britain and, as a mark of respect, every shop and business in Mullaghmore and Sligo closed down on the day the funeral processions passed through the County. I read somewhere recently that Prince Charles has expressed a wish that some day he might be able to visit Classiebawn Castle, where his uncle 'Dickie' spent so many happy holidays before his killers struck that August day in 1979.

3 'I KILLED HIM,' SAID THE BOY, AGED 11…

ALL KILLINGS are tragic but that of Matthew Coates was particularly so. He had survived two World Wars — then died at the hands of a tearaway teenager with a knife, at the age of 84. And to compound the tragedy, the person who discovered the body was his 77-year-old wife.

On 12 June 1984, Mr Coates had been brutally stabbed 12 times and left to die in a field near Clondalkin, Co. Dublin. The killing had taken place near a derelict house beside the Naas Road. As I lived in Clondalkin, I knew the area well.

A post mortem revealed that a stab wound to the neck had been fatal. He was already dead when his wife, a woman showing the frailty of her years, found him. The motive for the killing was unclear, as his belongings were untouched. His shocked wife confided: 'I always warned him not to talk to strangers or to interfere in anybody else's business.'

A building worker told us of seeing two youths walking along the Naas Road that afternoon. He did not like the look of them, he said, and was worried they might attempt to rob him. He had been relieved when they crossed the road and climbed over a wall. A man living nearby said he gave two youths a drink of water while a motorist offered matching descriptions of them and told us he saw them walking across the Naas Road around the time of the murder.

We were able to draw up descriptions of the youths, which we issued. Before long we had two suspects. A year before the killing two brothers were caught breaking into a parked chip van on the Naas Road. Then, just a month previously, the same two brothers were questioned about a break-in at a school in Clondalkin. People living in neighbouring houses saw them at the school and a garda detained them a short distance away and took their names and addresses. Their descriptions matched those of the youths seen on the Naas Road around the time of the murder. We identified them as 17-year-old John Doyle and his 11-year-old brother, Peter, from Tallaght, two miles from Clondalkin. They lived with their parents, seven brothers and two sisters in the family home. When detectives called to the house, John Doyle was asleep on the living-room floor while his young brother slept on a chair in his clothes, with an overcoat thrown over him.

The two were arrested on charges of malicious damage to property. We decided to separate them, with John being taken to Ronanstown Garda Station and his brother to Clondalkin. The 11-year-old immediately admitted killing Matthew Coates. It was a pathetically loyal attempt to help his older brother, but he made the mistake of telling us that after the killing he dropped the knife beside the body. That did not happen. The knife was not found near the body.

John Doyle finally confessed later that day. He said in his statement:

> I do not want my father to hear what I'm going to tell you now. Last Tuesday, myself and my brother left home around dinner time. We walked across the fields through Roadstone to Clondalkin. We were going to visit my uncle at the caravan site in Bawnogue, but changed our minds.
>
> We had a look around a few houses. We went for a walk around the place and I found a knife in the football field. It was like a hunting knife with an edge on one side of the blade. The handle was like hardwood with a shiny finish and carvings on it. I showed the knife to my brother and we went to a few more houses.
>
> We went to a house, I think it was near a bit of a farm, and asked a woman for water. She gave us a mug of water between the two of us. This woman lives in a house the far side of the Naas carriage-way from the chip van.
>
> We were cutting across home sometime after five o'clock. We cut across some wire beside the old broken down house. We were roaring and shouting at each other inside the old house for a while.

Then an old man came to the door of the house and started roaring and shouting at us. He was calling us bastards. He shouted: 'Get out of there, you bastards!'. We got afraid and my brother jumped out of the window. I tried to get out the door past him but he stopped me. I thought he had something in his hand and he was waving it at me.

I took out the knife I had in my left hand pocket. I swiped at him with the knife and he tried to hit me. He was backing away in front of me towards the avenue with the big trees on each side. I made a jab at him and the knife stuck in him. He grabbed a hold of me and he was shouting for help. I stabbed him a good few times with the knife. I was using the knife all the time with my left hand. I must have stabbed him at least a dozen times.

I then ran away after my brother down along the avenue towards the farmyard. I saw there was blood on the knife and I threw it away. Myself and Peter went home through the fields. I don't know what time we got home, but my older brother was home from work. Yesterday evening I saw in the Evening Herald that the man I stabbed was dead. I am sorry for killing the old man.

John Doyle was found guilty of manslaughter and spent three years in prison.

4 THE FATAL MISTAKE OF CAPTAIN NAIRAC...

THE BODY of Captain Robert Nairac, the undercover SAS man, murdered on the Border by the IRA, may never be discovered. Even the man who killed him, told me he does not know where it is, and I believe him.

He showed us the clothes he wore on the night of the killing, after Nairac had been seized while on a spying mission in South Armagh. He produced the captain's pistol — and the gun he had used to shoot him through the head. But he did not know what happened to the body, which was carried away by others after the murder and hidden.

Nairac, an officer in the Grenadier Guards and a member of the SAS — which glories in the motto, 'Who Dares Wins' — must have known the risks he was taking. Spying on the IRA in their South Armagh stronghold would be a highly dangerous mission even for a local man, let alone for someone with his background.

Could a former Oxford Blue (in boxing) really drink pints with the locals in a South Armagh pub, and attempt to sing Irish rebel songs, without attracting suspicion at what was one of the most violent periods in the Northern Troubles? Captain Nairac obviously thought he could. He was wrong — and the specially adapted Browning pistol which he carried, together with 50 rounds of ammunition, were not enough to save him.

The South Armagh Battalion of the IRA claimed responsibility for his killing. The man who actually pulled the trigger said later that he regretted the murder. He told us in his confession: 'I wish I'd never done it, no matter what he was or who he was. I don't believe I would ever have done it only I was full of drink, and that's telling the truth.'

Nairac had joined the British army while in his fourth year at Oxford, where he was reading history. He did his first tour in Northern Ireland in 1973. Then, after a special course with the army in Kenya, and now a captain, he volunteered to return to the North in April 1976. His South Armagh spying mission may have been foolhardy, but do not think this man was a 'soft target'. On the contrary the SAS is one of the toughest army units in the world and Captain Nairac would have been a trained expert at killing people himself.

I was called in to catch his killer because it was believed he lived south of the border. These political type cases were tense affairs, but the law is the law and my job was to enforce it. Many people at the time, both north and south of the Border, thought that we would not try very hard to catch those responsible. They were wrong. We never discriminated against anyone in these investigations, though this case was made more difficult by the fact that the British Army refused to co-operate and did not help us at any time during the investigation.

I learned later that Captain Nairac's commanding officer was furious that he had been allowed to go on a spying mission without the usual military back-up. On that Saturday, 14 May 1977, he had left the army base in Bessbrook, South Armagh, saying he was going on duty. He wore civilian clothes and drove a red Triumph car, the property of the Ministry of Defence. He told the base officer he was going to the Three Steps Inn public house in Drumintee, South Armagh, and later radioed from outside the pub that he was at his destination and would return to barracks by 11.30 p.m. He never did return. There were some indications that a person in the pub was a contact of Nairac's who was passing him on information.

The RUC made enquiries in the Three Steps, but everyone there was reluctant to say anything to them. They established that Capt Nairac drank some pints of beer and sang some rebel songs, accompanied by the small band playing in the pub that night. Later he was attacked in the car park outside. His red Triumph car was still there, the wing mirror broken. He had simply disappeared.

Four days later the first clue to his murder was discovered, south of the Border. Two men on their way to fish the Flurry River in Dundalk's

Ravensdale Park discovered two bullets and a small sum of money near the river bank. They also noticed some blood stains on the grass. The Gardaí were alerted.

We invited the RUC to come down and examine the scene, which they did. A number of items which we uncovered were sent for forensic examination. These included two shirt buttons, which appeared to have been ripped off as thread was still attached to them, and samples of head hair and dried blood. For comparison purposes, a sample of Captain Nairac's hair was obtained from his hairbrush at the barracks.

Then came a tip-off that a Liam Patrick Townson, who lived in Dundalk, might have been responsible for the murder. We found out that he was a 24-year-old carpenter who preferred to live in County Louth, though his family home was north of the Border, in Meigh, South Armagh.

He claimed he had left the North because he was afraid of the British Army. His father was a health inspector and his mother a nurse, and had four brothers and four sisters. The family was well respected in Meigh, and he appeared to be the 'black sheep'. Members of his family visited him while in custody and I was impressed by them.

I decided to bring him in for questioning. On 28 May he was arrested at a Garda/Army checkpoint on the Dundalk–Newry road and taken to Dundalk Garda Station. Two days later he subsequently made a full statement.

We were accused of extracting that statement by brutal means, but we never used violence of any nature in our interviews with suspects. At one stage, we allowed a doctor to visit him because he complained of a stomach upset. Anything a suspect wanted, within reason, was always provided. No case would stand up in court if violence was used during the interviews.

In his statement Townson said that on Saturday 14 May, the night of the murder, he had been drinking in Leonard's pub in Church Street, Dundalk, and later went to the Cabin public house in Bridge Street, where he stayed until 11.30 p.m. closing time.

> Someone from the Drumintee area came in and nodded at me to come out and I was talking to him at the door. He asked me could I get a gun. I asked him what he wanted it for, and he said they were holding some boy out the road. I asked him who he was and he said he thought it was a SAS soldier. He asked me would I go

out and I went out with him and someone from Jonesboro. I went out the road with the two boys in a car, which another man was driving, and picked up a revolver near the Border at a stone wall at the crossroads near Kilcurry. We then went down to Ravensdale and your man was there, that soldier. He was in a field beside the river just off the main road.

I went into the field and I asked somebody what the story was concerning that man. I asked them did they know anything about him, and I do not know which of them said he was acting suspiciously in the Three Steps Inn public house in Drumintee. They said he had introduced himself to some women as a Provo. They said he was carrying a gun in his holster and had a dud driving licence, and when he was asked about it, he said he got it off an uncle.

I asked where they got the gun and they said he pulled it on one of them outside the Three Steps Inn public house in Drumintee. When I got to the field first, Pat and Terry were in the field with him. Thomas and Jerry were there, too, standing on the road near the gateway beside the field. As I was crossing the field, there was a shot fired and I went into the field and shouted, 'watch that gun'. Somebody grabbed the gun from either Pat or the soldier. I don't know who it was and something fell into the river. I think it was a spare magazine for the soldier's gun.

When I went into the field, Pat handed me the gun and I pointed it into the air. I took him across the field then, from where he was standing against the bridge wall, and he tried to make a break for it. He was beaten and kicked then. I gave him a couple of thumps with my fist and I kicked him twice. There were three or four of us standing around and when he tried to make a break for it we all tried to hold him back.

He was knocked to the ground and I put the gun to his head and told him not to move. I asked him who he was and what was he doing in the Steps carrying a gun and claiming he was a Provo. He said he was Mickey somebody, I do not remember what he said his second name was, and that he was from Tennant Street, Belfast. I told him he was a liar and that he was an SAS soldier and I hit him a couple of times in the face with the butt of the gun. He was out in the field along the river bank at this time.

I asked him if he was a Provo and he did not answer. He just said Mickey something from Tennant Street in Belfast. I asked him again and he still did not answer. I asked him what he was doing in the Steps carrying a gun. I don't know what he said, and I told him if he did not tell me that he was a SAS soldier that I would shoot him. He said he was Mickey something from Tennant Street in Belfast. I asked him again and he said that he was a 'stickie'. I asked him who were the 'stickies' he knew in this area and he answered, 'Seamus from Drumintee', and I said: 'No you are wrong. He is not a stickie.'

I told him to get up, that we were heading for the North and that he would not be coming back. When we were coming to a ditch, he grabbed his own gun from my hand and I shouted: 'Come quick, he has the gun'. The two of us fell on the ground. Pat came forward and lifted a paling post and hit him a number of times across the head. That almost knocked him out. I again asked him again his name and he said Mickey whatever it was, and I told him that he was a British soldier and that I was going to shoot him.

I asked him did he want a priest and he mumbled something, I do not know what. Terry came over and I said: 'Let on you are a priest and see can you get any information from that man'.

He knelt down over him and blessed himself and we all stood back away out of the road. Terry talked to him for a few seconds. I do not know what he was saying. I took him away then and shot him in the head. The gun wasn't working right that I was using, so I clicked it a few times and then it went off.

I went back to the bridge where he was when I first came, to look for the spare magazine. I found it beside a stone. I went to everyone that was there near the gate and told them that if there was a man done for this, I would use the gun again. After I told them not to mention it to anyone, I went across the fields with two fellows and the other boys went away by car.

The three of us changed our clothes. I gave them some of my clothes. I gathered up the clothes, along with the two weapons, and went down to the yard. I put the clothes in a white box and went away to hide them. The two boys went away up the road walking. I think they were heading for Dundalk. I went back to the house and went to bed.

> I wish I'd never done it, no matter what he was or who he was.
> I don't believe I would ever have done it only I was full of drink,
> and that's telling the truth.

Townson was then taken in handcuffs to show detectives where he had hidden the guns and clothing. A white box containing shoes and clothing were found under a pile of loose stones on a back road on the way to Dromad. Further on the guns were recovered in a bag, which was concealed under a stone at the foot of a tree. Townson even warned the detectives to be careful as he was not sure what condition they were in. The bag contained two guns. Townson said: 'That is my gun, the other one is the captain's. The bag also contained a holster and some rounds of ammunition.

Later that day, Liam Townson also showed us where he had collected the gun on the night he killed Captain Nairac.

As we tied up the loose ends of the case, we were able to piece together the events of the night that ended in murder. Captain Nairac had gone to the Three Steps Inn and ordered a pint, mingling with the other customers and chatting to different people. He ordered another drink and then asked the band if he could sing some rebel songs. They had no objection, so he did so. He was unaware that at least seven people in the pub suspected he was an undercover SAS soldier. He changed his background story twice, and that was to be his downfall, together with the fact that he could not sing the songs properly.

As he was talking to an old man near the bar, he was pointed out to some IRA supporters who noted his every move. One of them went over and whispered something to Captain Nairac, who agreed to go out to the car park with him. Three or four other men followed him.

In the car park a scuffle broke out. Nairac was kicked to the ground and one of the men held him down by the throat. In the struggle he had dropped his service revolver. That lay on the ground, out of his reach, as he desperately searched for it with his free hand. One of the men picked up the gun and put it to his head, warning: 'Don't move, you fucker, or I'll shoot you.'

A man, driving a Ford Cortina, pulled up beside them and by kicking and pulling his hair, they managed to force Nairac on to the car floor. The gun was stuck in his back as the vehicle sped away. They took him to Ravensdale Bridge, then dragged him from the Cortina and into the field.

As they waited for Townson to come with the gun and interrogate him, they beat the prisoner. Every time he struggled they kicked and punched him until he didn't move anymore. He sat there, his hands over his face, waiting. He still had his senses about him, and he must have known that what he was waiting for was death.

One of the two guns that Townson had helped us find was Nairac's Browning semi-automatic pistol. He had made some adjustments to it, so that it could be concealed more easily under his jacket and pulled quickly from its underarm holster in emergencies.

The theory was good but in practice he had dropped the Browning automatic during the melee in the car park of the Three Steps Inn. That night he had left his other revolver in the barracks.

The gun which Townson identified as his was a Barrington and Richardson revolver, a .32 inch calibre. Though it was capable of firing a bullet, it had two faults, which explained why Townson said it 'clicked' a few times before the fatal shooting. The two spent cases found at Ravensdale were confirmed as having been fired by the Harrington and Richardson revolver.

I was satisfied that Liam Townson, with the help of accomplices, had murdered Captain Nairac. While in our custody, he was absolutely certain that he was going to be hanged if found guilty. We had a hard task convincing him that the penalty for murder was imprisonment. He said he would rather tear his own heart out than face the hangman.

The trial took place in the Special Criminal Court in Dublin in November 1977 and Townson was found guilty of the murder and sentenced to penal servitude for life.

The RUC and the British Government thanked us for our help in solving the case. He was released in August 1990.

Despite the fact that the man who killed Captain Nairac did not know where the body was buried, some local members of the Provisional IRA did. There were hopes during the IRA ceasefire of 31 August 1994 that the Gardaí would be told of the exact location so that his remains could be taken home for burial.

A number of other members of the IRA were charged with the murder in the North. Two fled the area immediately after the killing and are believed to be in the United States.

5 WHEN HUSBANDS ARE SUSPECTS...

WHENEVER THE pressures of the job got to me during my years in the Murder Squad, I would round up my family and head for Annascaul, Co. Kerry. Inch beach is about three miles long and I would jog or stroll along the shoreline, savouring the tranquil atmosphere. I had no phone there, but invariably the local officer would call to my house and tell me I had to contact Garda Headquarters in Dublin. On 29 December 1981, we were in Annascaul for the Christmas holiday when such a call came. I packed my bags and travelled to Monasterevin to investigate a suspicious car accident in which a woman driver had died.

Anne Holmes, who was 34, had been found in her Datsun car, which was embedded in a ditch one mile from her home and close to Coolnaferragh Bog, on the Portarlington to Monasterevin Road. Initial examination of the scene suggested she may had suffered a blackout or seizure and lost control of the vehicle, which then spun off the road. There was glass on her body from a smashed window on the driver's side and her head was badly gashed. So serious was the injury that she would have died almost immediately.

Her husband, Henry Holmes, was understandably very distressed about her death. He owned a knitwear factory at Ballybrittas and when Sergeant James O'Halloran called to the factory and told him about the accident, he collapsed in shock.

When I inspected the accident scene I noticed that Mrs Holmes's car had entered the ditch at a right angle to the road. This was not consistent with the idea of her suddenly losing control of her car. If that had happened, the car would have veered off the road.

I was not satisfied with the situation. I felt that someone else had a hand in what happened. My suspicion was that the car had stopped before someone turned the steering wheel sharply to the right, pushing it into the ditch with Mrs Holmes sitting in the driver's seat.

Assistant State Pathologist Dr Gilsenan, who conducted the post mortem, also felt that the head injury was too severe to have been caused by the accident. The woman also had abrasions on her neck, head and shoulders, which he found hard to explain in the circumstances. One of her eyes had been blackened by what he believed was a single, separate blow, possibly a punch. That suspicion of foul play was confirmed when a blood-stained lump hammer was discovered concealed in another vehicle parked outside the family home.

The evidence pointed to murder. I began a thorough investigation of her movements, her friends and, most of all, of her husband. I had no reason to suspect him but experience had taught me that the husband is often the culprit when a woman meets her death in the family home. In this case, Anne Holmes had been found only a mile from her home. In murder cases where a wife is killed, my policy was always to check the husband first, and either eliminate him completely, or concentrate all my investgative efforts on him.

The first step was to find out how the couple got on together and if either was having an affair. Henry Holmes, we found, had not been getting on too well with his wife, though he did enjoy himself in the company of his factory staff.

His display of emotion over his wife's death did not influence my thinking. I never let emotions affect my judgement during investigations. Hard, cold facts were what counted. That may sound harsh, but after years of working face to face with death and violence you learn to get on with the job. You have to adopt a 'tunnel vision' approach in the hunt for a killer. Nothing must be allowed to divert your attention.

Henry Holmes did not have a strong alibi for the afternoon of the murder. My men discovered that he had lied about his movements. He was definitely the No.1 suspect. However, I have never been overly influenced by alibis, one way or the other. I was always suspicious of a person who could give me a detailed account of his or her movements without hesitating. It is almost impossible, even for a person with a reasonable memory, to recall exactly what they did at a given time a few days ago. In many cases, where people being questioned gave me precise details of their actions at the time when a crime was committed, I was even more suspicious of them.

Henry Holmes did not visit the local church where his wife's remains lay and this surprised and shocked most of the local mourners. I had him brought in for further questioning. My instincts told me that he was the killer. So did the facts. Finally, in the course of the interrogation he admitted to Detective Sergeant Gerry O'Carroll and Detective Sergeant Tom Connolly that he had killed his wife.

He told us that he was laying linoleum in their kitchen while his wife watched. He was having difficulty putting it down properly and was feeling the strain. His wife said he was not doing a good job. It was a remark that cost her her life. His temper snapped and he beat her across the head with the lump hammer he was using at the time, killing her.

When he realised what he had done, he panicked, dragged her body to the car and drove out the Portarlington Road. Once he had found a likely spot, he put her in the driving seat and pushed the car into the ditch. He then returned home for a short while before setting off for his knitwear factory. It was there, some hours later, that he collapsed when told of his wife's death.

I have always been shocked by the violence which some men use against their wives and girlfriends. And I have always felt that women should notify the Gardaí immediately such attacks start. While doing a refresher course in New Scotland Yard, I was impressed by the approach of English police, who take photographs of the injuries received by women in domestic violence when dealing with such cases.

If women are assaulted, verbally or otherwise, and if they intend to stay with the perpetrator of the crime, they should always inform their local Gardaí of the situation. They can caution the attacker or, in extreme cases, issue court proceedings. Many relationships improve following involvement by the Gardaí. If not, then the details of previous assaults will be on file.

On 19 September 1982, Henry Holmes was found not guilty of murder but guilty of manslaughter, and sentenced to 10 years imprisonment. The saddest aspect of the case was the confirmation that his wife was pregnant when he battered her to death in the kitchen of their home.

6   GARDA KILLERS AND THE DEATH PENALTY...

I HAVE WRITTEN elsewhere in this book that all murders are investigated with the same degree of vigour and determination. That is not entirely true. There is one type of murder which provokes a greater emotional commitment from the Force — the killing of a Garda colleague, especially in the line of duty.

Such killings have been capital offences, carrying a death penalty. But in all such cases over the past 30 years, those convicted have had their sentences reduced to life imprisonment, however flimsy the defence they offered. It made me wonder why we had not abolished the offence of capital murder and the penalty prescribed for it.

Would capital punishment, if implemented, have made a difference in the number of gardaí who have been murdered over the years? Who can say? What I do know is that if I had been asked my views on the death penalty, in the immediate aftermath of the cold-blooded killing of Detective Garda John Morley and Garda Henry Byrne in Ballaghadereen, Co. Roscommon, in July 1980, I would have said I fully supported it. However, months later, when the killers were behind bars, my anger had cooled and I had changed my mind. I do not believe that the death penalty would solve anything. In fact, I can see situations in which it would make matters worse. If, for instance, those who had murdered a garda, knew for certain that they would be hanged if caught, how many others might they butcher to ensure their escape?

The double Garda killing, described by the then Commissioner, Patrick McLaughlin as the worst case of murder in the history of the State, had started with a bank robbery. On 7 July 1980, three armed and masked men raided the Bank of Ireland in Ballaghadereen taking £46,500. They fired a number of shots during the robbery, but luckily no one was injured. Two local gardaí who drove to the scene were held at gunpoint by the raiders who immobilised their patrol car and broke their radio, before driving off in a white Ford Cortina.

Castlerea Station sent a patrol car to intercept the Cortina. Aboard were Garda Glen O'Kelly, Detective Garda John Morley, Garda Henry Byrne and Sergeant M. O'Malley. Garda Morley was armed with an Uzi machine gun.

By sheer chance, the patrol car collided with the Cortina at Shannon Cross. One of the raiders immediately jumped out and sprayed the Garda vehicle with bullets. The windscreen shattered and Garda Byrne died instantly from gunshot wounds. Though seated in the back of the patrol car, he was the only garda to be struck by the bullets.

The raiders then reversed the Cortina away from the patrol car, with gardaí O'Kelly and Morley giving chase on foot. The robbers soon abandoned the car and two of them ran through a field parallel to the road, while the third man raced away over fields in the opposite direction. Garda Morley fired warning bursts over the hedge, but some shots rang out and he fell to the ground. He died later from the gunshot wounds.

The bank raiders escaped, leaving a scene of carnage behind them.

My boss, Commissioner McLaughlin, directed me to go to Castlerea and take charge of the murder investigation. He followed me down that afternoon. The then Taoiseach, Charles Haughey, and Justice Minister Gerry Collins also arrived. Mr Haughey asked me if I required anything to help in the investigation. I thanked him and gave an assurance that the perpetrators would not remain free for long.

Every garda in the entire country wanted to be a member of this investigation. They were shocked and disgusted by the cowardly and merciless actions of the bank robbers.

Gardaí Henry Byrne and John Morley, a County GAA star, were from Knock, Co. Mayo, and were buried there. Colleagues travelled from all over Ireland to attend their funerals, the largest ever seen in Knock. Every GAA County Board showed their respect for the murdered policemen. At the Connacht Final, a minute's silence was requested and a moving tribute paid to the men.

The murders cast a shadow of grief and shock over their home county. John Morley was a popular Gaelic football star, who played centre-half-back for his county and had given many stirring displays. Henry Byrne, an equally popular and respected member of the community, was also sorely missed. Messages of sympathy flooded in to their wives and families.

I tried to push my emotional feelings aside. I had a job to do — to catch the killers, both for the sake of the gardaí and the law-abiding citizens of Ireland.

A special team was set up to comb back-roads which the raiders may have used in their escape. There was an early success. The team found a young man lying injured near Derrycahan Wood, a farmland area, about 10 miles from the scene of the shootings. His clothing was blood-stained and he appeared to have a chest injury. He said he had been shot in an accident and identified himself as a Mr O'Shea from Cork City. Although the team questioned him intensively, he refused to give any further information.

He was taken to Tuam hospital for treatment and from there to Galway Regional Hospital. I ordered a round-the-clock guard on him in case of a rescue attempt. After he recovered, we arrested him under Section 30 of the Offences Against the State Act, 1939, and subsequently he was charged with murder.

I was satisfied that O'Shea was one of the three-men gang though he would not admit to anything, or give us any details about the other two.

The leg work began. I always conducted searches of this scale along the lines of an army commander. Detailed maps were pinned on the walls and the search parties were made aware of the main physical features of the different areas being checked. I organised over 100 gardaí into different groups, and each day they combed different regions marked out on the map. The search was a huge drain on Garda resources as members of the force were required from as far away as Belmullet, Co. Mayo.

At the end of each day, the area searched was marked on the Ordinance Survey map and the next area to be searched indicated with a different colour. This ensured no repetition. The sergeant in charge of each search party accounted for the region he checked. Road blocks were maintained in case the fugitives were flushed from their hiding places.

Our methods proved successful. One of the murderers had taken refuge in some fields after the shooting. He was stopped at a checkpoint at French Park on the morning of 9 July. He was identified as Patrick McCann, taken into custody and subsequently charged with murder.

The Forensic team checked the two vehicles involved during the shootings. A number of bullet holes were found in the patrol car. Glass fragments and paint samples were collected to compare with those found in O'Shea's shirt and jacket. They matched.

The Forensic team also discovered a footprint on the counter in the Bank of Ireland premises in Ballaghdereen. In a murder trial it is far better to have the piece of evidence with the print in court rather than just a photograph. I sent two detectives to the bank to take the counter away. The bank manager graciously gave them permission to do so. As usual, Dr Jim Donovan of the Forensic team did a brilliant job.

We had one more fugitive to apprehend. The search was stepped up and extended to Co. Galway. Intensive enquiries revealed that a man named Peter Pringle was in hiding in Galway and that he could be the man that we sought. I must point out that the two suspects we had in custody by this stage did not give us any information about accomplices.

We believed that Peter Pringle, heavily bearded by now, had bought some sweets in a shop some miles from the scene of the murders, and the shopkeeper, and a customer who happened to be the local garda's wife, had become suspicious of him. She told her husband, Garda Boyle, who tried to intercept him, but was unsuccessful. We subsequently learnt that he had hijacked a lorry and managed to pass through the checkpoints.

Now our attention was mainly focused on Co. Galway. Peter Pringle was our main suspect, so I ordered that all his previous associates and friends be kept under constant surveillance. My information was that Pringle was still in Galway City. I was right. On 19 July we finally caught him. He had followed the usual pattern for a man on the run. Most fugitives tend to keep in contact with their girlfriends, usually to the exclusion of all others. We had kept his girlfriend under continuous surveillance. Unknowingly, she led detectives to a house at Ballybane near the Galway Racecourse — and to Pringle.

He was escorted to Galway Station and detained under Section 30 of the Offences Against the State Act, 1939. Later he was charged with one of the Garda's murders, a capital offence.

At the trial the evidence we produced against the accused included the counter from the Bank of Ireland in Ballaghadereen with O'Shea's footprint upon it. The case we had against them was too much for their defence team. On 27 November 1980, they were convicted in the Special Criminal Court in Dublin.

The presiding Judge read out the sentence: 'That you, on the 7th day of July 1980, murdered one Henry Byrne, a member of the Gardaí acting in the course of his duty, that the three of you be detained in custody and that on the 19th of December 1980, the three of you suffer death by execution in the manner prescribed by law and that after such a sentence shall have been carried into effect, the three bodies shall be buried within the precincts of the said prison.'

As usual, after much deliberation and delays, the sentences were commuted to life imprisonment, 15 years, to date from 27 November 1980.

We had won a hollow victory against the men who murdered our colleagues, Henry Byrne and John Morley. Garda Morley has a son in the Gardaí who is stationed in Galway.

As for the money, the £46,500 taken in the robbery was fully recovered. It was still in the boot of the gang's getaway Ford Cortina, the vehicle into which the Garda patrol had crashed with such tragic consequences.

In May of 1995, the Court of Criminal Appeal quashed the murder conviction against Peter Pringle. It accepted new evidence that there had been a conflict of testimony between the two gardaí at his trial, which cast doubt on the authenticity of his alleged admission of involvement in the crime.

Mr Pringle had never made a written confession. He had served 15 years of the life sentence when released.

7　A KILLER TRAPPED
　　　BY HIS SPECTACLES...

CRIME WRITERS use a variety of ploys to unmask their villain in the final chapter. It may be a missing shirt button, an unused train ticket or a half-smoked cigarette from a distinctive brand which enables the fictional super sleuth to tie up all the loose ends and slip the handcuffs on the guilty party.

In the case of real-life killer Michael Flynn, fact almost matched fiction — he was a murderer who was brought to justice by his spectacles. And the discovery of the glasses, which proved to be the crucial clue, underlined once again the absolute importance of preserving the crime scene.

That's the police jargon for it. What it means in layman's language is simply this: Don't touch anything or move anything in the immediate area in which a crime has been committed until the police officers arrive — and don't let anyone else do it either. That was the approach adopted by security guard Walter Denton when a young woman's body was discovered in a lane off Dublin's Kirwan Street on 25 September 1983.

His presence of mind was to be a vital factor in the success of the subsequent investigation.

The two boys, aged 5 and 6, who found the body assumed the girl was drunk. They told their mother and the Gardaí were alerted.

Mr Denton, who lived on Kirwan Street, liked listening to police radio transmissions on his VHF set. That morning he was intrigued by a message to a Bridewell patrol car to go to the lane off Kirwan Street to help a sick woman there. He knew the lane was a dead-end, so there was no reason for anyone to walk down there at that time of the morning. He decided to investigate.

A small group of women were standing at the entrance to the lane, seemingly reluctant to go any further. Mr Denton edged past them and then saw various personal items scattered around the body of Denise Flanagan. He immediately walked back to the lane entrance and took up station so as to preserve the scene of the crime. He would not let the women past him when they wanted to cover up the girl's body.

When an ambulance arrived, he directed the crew down the lane. As they reached the corpse, one of the men was about to step on a pair of spectacles lying nearby. Walter Denton intervened and pulled him aside. State Pathologist, Dr John Harbison, reported that the woman had been strangled. Her personal effects lay strewn about the alleyway and it was obvious she had put up a hell of a struggle against her attacker.

Denis Flanagan later identified his daughter Denise. His wife had had a premonition that morning when she heard a girl's body had been discovered. She was certain it was their daughter.

The Flanagan family lived on Stanhope Street, a short distance from the murder scene. When Denise had not returned home that night, her mother phoned the hospital where she worked to see if she had gone directly there. She hadn't and Mrs Flanagan became increasingly worried about her safety. Her husband alerted the Gardaí .

I was in charge of the Murder Squad at the time and I was assisted by Superintendent William J. Herlihy and Detective Dick Walsh in the investigation. When I arrived at the scene I first checked, as I always did in such circumstances, if the victim had been anointed. She had not, so I sent for the local priest who carried out the last rites.

I was then ready to begin the investigation. Friends, neighbours and members of the public enabled us to piece together Denise Flanagan's movements on the night she died.

She had left home at 6 p.m., going first to her friend Ruth's house. At 7.05 p.m. they went to the Rainbow Disco in Exchequer Street where she danced with some boys and enjoyed the night. At pub closing time Ruth said she was going home with her boyfriend and Denise told her she would make her own way home.

She went on to Rumours Disco at midnight where she met an acquaintance, Patricia Ruane. She joined Patricia and her brother for a while and then left the disco alone. It was shortly before 2 a.m.

Around 2.30 a.m., Patricia, who had gone with her brother and some friends to the Burger King Restaurant in O'Connell Street, some 50 yards from Rumours, spotted Denise at a nearby table. She was chatting to a young man. Patricia was able to give us a good description of the man — including the fact that he wasn't wearing spectacles.

They shouted over to Denise and joked with her. At 3 a.m. when Patricia and her party left Burger King, Denise and the man were still there.

Some 10 minutes later, Burger King doorman, Michael Dunne, wanted to clear up and asked the customers to leave. Denise and the young man walked off towards O'Connell Bridge. Patricia and her friends spotted them again. She spoke to Denise and her brother kissed her. Then Denise and the man got into a taxi.

The car belonged to Peter 'Pep' Byrne. He told us that Denise asked to be taken to Manor Street, but he got the impression that there were to be two drops, her first and then her companion at another destination. As he drove, the couple were embracing in the back of the car.

At Manor Street, Denise Flanagan got out of the taxi and the young man moved to get out as well. He paid the fare and as he got out Denise asked him: 'Are you not staying on?' He replied 'No.' Mr Byrne saw them walking across Manor Street and into Kirwan Street. Apart from her killer, he was the last person to see Denise Flanagan alive.

It was at this stage I decided to concentrate the investigation on the pair of spectacles found at the murder scene and which the ambulance man had almost trodden underfoot. I enlisted the help of Brendan Culleton, a director of Optics International Ltd and one of the leading opticians in Ireland, to try to identify the owner. His company supplied ophthalmic goods to the profession.

The spectacles were the Bailen brand, made by Barbudo of Madrid, with a B.H. colour code. The frames were 560/4. The lenses were pear shaped and cut from 65mm. lenses. They were found to have an 0.50D (D = Dioptic) sight correction on each and they had the slightest possible tint, known as B.15 tint, or Ist tint. Mr Culleton confirmed that his company supplied many opticians with this particular model and, significantly, that the spectacles we had found were relatively new.

They didn't belong to Denise, she didn't wear glasses. That left only her killer. Now the 'leg work' really began. There is no central computer which can reveal the names of those who wear a particular type of glasses. One by one, every optician in Dublin was visited and their records checked. That failed to find the owner, so we extended the search to Dublin County and finally to the whole of Ireland. More than 247,000 individual records were checked. We were looking for anyone who had been supplied with spectacles which either had Bailen frames or lenses with a + 0.50D sight correction.

Fifteen days after the murder of Denise Flanagan, Detective Martin Thompson called to optician Angela O'Neill of Blanchardstown and told her what we were looking for. The next day she phoned to say she had a prescription which seemed to fit our requirements. The prescription was for Michael Flynn, of Blanchardstown, Dublin. It was the breakthrough we had been hoping for in the investigation.

Michael Flynn was 23 and a part-time worker with a firm making aluminium windows. He was arrested by Detective Sergeant Tony Hickey and Detective Garda Gerry Nolan and brought to Bridewell Garda Station. He told us he had lost the spectacles at Rumours Disco some weeks ago. He began to shake and asked a detective for a cigarette. He admitted that he had met a girl in the Burger King restaurant on the night of the murder and agreed to make a full statement.

> On Saturday night, two weeks ago, I went on my own to Rumours Disco in O'Connell Street. I had tried to get into Heartbreaks in the Phoenix Park first, but I didn't get in as the place seemed to be full. I got into Rumours between half twelve and a quarter to one. I had a few drinks there. I had earlier had a few drinks in Davy and Phelan in Blanchardstown, with my brother John.
>
> In Rumours I was talking to the piano player, I think his name is Max, and to a girl that sings there sometimes. I think her name is Jackie. I was dancing on my own at the edge of the floor and I got in for a while with a group who were also dancing. I spoke to a girl, who told me she was from Terenure and I told her that I was from Blanchardstown. I was wearing my glasses and they fell off me a few times during the night. I then put them in the breast pocket of my jacket. I got these glasses about a year ago in the opticians at the Health Centre in Blanchardstown. They are tinted with brown frames and with a few scratches on one of the lenses.
>
> I left the disco on my own when it was finished at about two o'clock. I went to Burger King on the corner in O'Connell Street. I had a cup of coffee and chips.

I sat on a seat with my back to the door. There was this girl sitting facing me. I did not know her. She may have just finished eating. I think her bag was on the table. After a few minutes, she asked me if I had a cigarette. I gave her a cigarette. She asked me where I was from and I told her. She told me she worked in a hospital and she asked me where I worked.

We were almost the last to leave, and the doorman came over and passed some friendly remark to us. On O'Connell Street she asked me how I was getting home. I told her I was getting a taxi. She asked: 'Will that go by Manor Street?' We agreed to go together in a taxi.

As we walked from the burger place towards North Earl Street, she met some people she seemed to know. They were fellows and at least one girl. She was talking to them and she kissed one of the fellows. I stayed in the background as I did not know them. We walked to the island in the middle of O'Connell Street and got a taxi to Manor Street. In the back of the taxi we had our arms around each other, and kissed each other several times. She told the driver to go to Manor Street and stopped him near the pedestrian crossing. I paid the taxi, I think it was a few quid. We walked across Manor Street and straight down another street opposite us. We came to a laneway on the right hand side.

We stopped there and had a cigarette. We then had a court. We moved up the lane a bit, and the same thing happened again. She was coming on fairly heavy and seemed to be happy to go up the lane. We went right to the end of the lane. I was worked up and my hands were all over her. When I put my hand on her private part she said 'No.' I continued and the next thing my hands were around her neck and she was trying to get her feet up to kick me.

She was struggling like mad, she probably knew that I was going to kill her or hurt her seriously. She seemed to pass out. Her feet were towards the wall with her head towards the street and she was on her back.

I got up and fixed up my clothes. I walked to the end of the lane. I saw her bag on the lane. I walked into Manor Street and on to Hanlon's Corner. I walked beyond Cabra Cross and got a taxi between the labour exchange and the police station. I think the taximan lives somewhere in the area, he said something about going home. I sat in the front seat and got out at the shopping centre in Blanchardstown, beyond my own road. I got home and went to bed. All the family were in bed.

I got up at half past twelve the next day, Sunday. I was sick and I hoped what had happened to me was a dream. That evening I heard the whole lot on the news, that the girl had been found strangled and I heard her name for the first time. It was Denise Flanagan. I was going to go to the police station. I was going to go to Confession and I was going to ring the Samaritans but I did not. I was going to commit suicide by jumping in front of a train. I was worried about the effect on my family, and I still am.

Michael Flynn was charged with the murder of Denise Flanagan. Before he was taken away to Mountjoy Prison, he told us what clothes he was wearing on the night of the murder and he also allowed us to fingerprint him. As a piece of further evidence, with the help of Dr Barry, a leading orthodontist, we were able to link the bite marks on Denise Flanagan's body with her killer. Dr Barry was entirely satisfied that the moulds he took of Flynn's mouth and teeth matched the marks exactly. It was the first time that this technique had been used in Ireland.

From the window of the squad car he saw his parents entering the Bridewell station as we were about to leave for the jail. He said he would like to speak to them. His mother and father got into the car. His mother said: 'You didn't do this son. Tell mama the truth.'

She repeated this. Her son replied 'I was there that night, I was with that girl. I don't know what happened.' His mother said: 'We will stand by you.' His parents got out of the car and we took him to Mountjoy Jail.

At the subsequent trial, Michael Flynn was found guilty of the murder of Denise Flanagan and sentenced to penal servitude for life in April 1985. He was released in July 1995.

The preservation of the scene of the crime by Walter Denton had been invaluable to our investigation, as the pair of spectacles was the only clue left behind by the killer. It was the first investigation, I later learned, in which a murderer had been identified by his glasses.

8 'I AM NOT JACK THE RIPPER'...

IT WAS a murder that was both savage and apparently motiveless: a young girl chosen at random by a total stranger and brutally stabbed to death in front of two horrified school friends.

The bizarre killing of 8-year-old Colette Cronin on 2 May 1974, as she picked flowers with her friends in the Lehenaghmore area of Togher, a Cork city suburb, shocked and frightened parents throughout Ireland. If a murderer stalked such an unlikely place, could their children be safe anywhere?

For Colette's pals, 10-year-old Pauline O'Rourke and Alexandra O'Donovan, aged 9, Lehenaghmore was a favourite spot for gathering flowers. They had been there several times before. That afternoon, following school, Colette agreed to go with them. It was a decision which was to cost her her life.

They were on their way home, bunches of flowers in hand, when they saw the killer. He was standing at the door of a derelict building, known locally as Trampas House because tramps occasionally slept there. He was in his thirties, Pauline O'Rourke later recalled, short and skinny, with untidy hair, a pimply face and a moustache that appeared to be struggling to grow. As they passed, he muttered hello in what seemed to her an unusual accent. It was the only word he spoke.

Then, without warning, he seized Colette from behind and dragged her into the derelict house. In a few frenzied seconds, as she struggled and cried for help, he ended her young life with a hunting knife, stabbing her six times in the stomach.

Her friends, too stunned to realise the awfulness of what had happened, ran to raise the alarm. The killer fled too, racing across a field at the back of the house and disappearing.

Who was he? What possible motive could there be for such a random and savage killing?

As I arrived from Dublin with the Murder Squad to begin the investigation, parents in the area were frantic with worry, fearing that he could strike again. I could understand their feelings. I had five children myself, including two girls, and this savage crime disgusted me.

Four days into the investigation, a note discovered in a Cork church, addressed to the Garda, gave the first glimpse into the mind of the person we were hunting. 'I was present at the derelict house,' it said. 'I was actually made to kill the little girl by two men.'

Two days later, another note arrived. 'I am not Jack the Ripper,' it said. 'I am innocent.' By now I knew for certain that the man we were seeking was a very disturbed individual.

But the story of this investigation really starts with Pauline O'Rourke, the child who saw her young friend murdered. The day after the killing she described what happened.

> We knew we would get flowers by the railway line and at the back of Trampas House. We had gone there five or six times before, but sometimes Colette did not come. We passed by the fruit factory and there were only a few cars there. We passed Trampas House and we looked into it but did not go in. It was 3.30 p.m. There was nobody in the house.
>
> We continued on up to the bridge. We stayed around up there about half an hour. I said we will go home now, it will be getting dark soon. When we got to the road, we walked straight down the hill. We could see Trampas House. There was a man standing at the door. He was still standing by the house as we were passing.
>
> He was in his thirties, about 33. His hair was cut short. It was straight but his fringe was a bit curly. He had a moustache, but there was not much hair in it. It was all grey. He was skinny and smaller than my dad. My dad is 5 ft 4 ins. He was wearing a dark grey suit. It was clean and sort of new. His hair was a bit untidy and some of it was standing up at the back. He had a few pimples on his left cheek.

As we were passing he said 'Hello' to us. He spoke with a strange tone. I thought it was English. Colette was about five or ten yards behind us. We looked back and the man put his hands around Colette. He ran into the kitchen and laid her down and knelt down next to her. She was lying on her back on the floor.

We were looking in the door. The man did not see us as his back was turned to us. Colette kept calling all the time, 'Alex get help'. He was holding her two knees together and I saw him put his hand into his right hand trouser pocket and take out something. I did not see what he took out. When we saw him do this we ran away. We ran down to the fruit factory through the field.

I saw the man run out the back door of the house and straight through the field at the back. We went into the factory and called the men. We saw one of them lifting Colette out of the house. There was blood on her knees. I never saw the man before. I would know him if I saw him again.

The stranger had stabbed Colette six times in the abdomen in a frenzied attack. The postmortem revealed that she bled to death.

As the investigation got under way, people living near the scene of the killing were questioned. A lot of the locals had spotted the suspect and we had accurate descriptions of him. We also located the murder weapon underneath the floorboards of Trampas House, a blood-stained hunting knife.

All the material evidence was sent to the Forensic Laboratory in Dublin and the hunt for the killer, who had escaped from the area, began in earnest.

Four days after the murder, Derry Maher, a school attendance officer, made an unusual discovery as he was leaving St Vincent's Church, Sundays Well, Cork, having dropped in to say a quick prayer. Just inside the door, he noticed a white envelope marked 'Urgent Garda'. He alerted a local and together they read the note. It said:

I was present at the derelict house at Doughclayne on that terrible day of the murder. I was actually made to kill the little girl by two men. Apparently their reason was to frame me. I am in a state of shock. I am very frightened. Tell the little girl's parents I am heartily sorry. Please make a plea to me. Try to assure me I will be all right if I come in. I need love.

The letter was passed on to us and we, in turn, dispatched it and the envelope to the Forensic Section. The pressure for an arrest was now increasing, especially from parents of young children. I didn't mind the pressure. Every murder investigation is fraught with tension and anxiety. I was at my best in such situations.

I felt the killing was the work of a man who was mentally disturbed and began to check on all out-patients of Cork Mental Hospital. Most of the out-patients were either incoherent or unstable. During the days that followed we spoke to, and assessed, many of the 136 interviewed. It was tough going.

One man interviewed, at Barrack Street Garda Station, was very nervous. I ordered a check on his 'family tree' — an expression I always used when asking about a person's background — and was told he had a brother who was a mental hospital outpatient.

Detective Sergeant Paul Downing went to interview the man's brother, but he was not at home. The detective told his mother that he wanted to interview him in connection with the murder of Colette Cronin, and to fingerprint him. He called to the house a second time on my instructions, but without any luck. Unknowingly, however, he had flushed the murderer into the open. I subsequently learned that his mother had told him that they wanted to interview him in relation to a murder.

Six days into the investigation another note arrived. It was found by Maeve O'Sullivan, a science student at UCC, on the footpath near Glendalough Park. She brought the blue envelope, with the word 'Garda' on it to Togher Garda Station. It read:

It's me again. I told you what happened. It's true. No, I am not Jack the Ripper. I am innocent.

As with the previous note, this was also forwarded to the Forensic Section for analysis.

Next day there was a third note, discovered this time by 16-year-old Marian Conway, from Ballylean, Cork, near Donovan's Road. The wording was familiar:

It's me again. I am very sick. Did you catch the two men?

That was followed by a phonecall. Garda Michael O'Rourke took it at Cork's Union Quay Station. 'You know what happened in the woods in

Togher,' said the male caller. 'I was there. I was at the scene. I was made to kill her. Two people made me do it. I had to kill her. They made me do it.'

Garda O'Rourke attempted to keep the man talking while efforts were made to trace the call. It was eventually traced to a public kiosk at the UCC gates, but the man had fled before the patrol car arrived.

That same evening a man approached nurse Irene Donnelly at reception in Cork's South Infirmary Hospital and asked to see a doctor. He looked nervous and said he had a pain in his chest.

In the accident room he told a Dr Lucey he was in a state of shock. Asked why he was shocked, he replied 'you would be, too, if you had killed the girl in Togher'. Then he said he had written letters to the Gardaí but they had ignored them. Dr Lucey encouraged the man to lie on a couch and whispered to a nurse to telephone the Gardaí. The man said the Gardaí had found the knife, that his fingerprints were on it and that once they obtained his fingerprints they would know he was the culprit. Without any prompting, he added that he had thrown the knife under the floorboards. When asked his name, he replied, Tobin, but would not give his Christian name.

Dr Lucey asked him if he was ever in hospital before and he mumbled something about a mental hospital in England. He then mentioned the mental hospital in Cork and that he was afraid the doctor would send him there. Dr Lucey then said he had informed the Gardaí and the man got to his feet and rushed from the hospital.

The doctor and an assistant followed him down Infirmary Road. Luck was with them. A patrol car came around the corner and the doctor flagged it down. The man, when apprehended, told the gardaí his name was Anthony Tobin and asked where they were taking him. They told him Barrack Street Garda Station and he said: 'Oh good, not to the mental home'.

The interrogation did not take long. On 10 May, just over a week after the killing, Francis Anthony Tobin made a full confession. He admitted buying a knife at the Gun Stores in Oliver Plunkett St., Cork, for £1, having collected his dole money. At first he claimed, as he had done in the notes, that two men in the derelict house had forced him to kill the girl. However, in a subsequent statement, he gave a different version.

> About two years ago I had a nervous breakdown in London because I could not find a place and I had to live out in the open. I

came back to Ireland and I was taken against my wishes by two psychiatric nurses to St Anne's Hospital. I kicked up a fuss and they sent for three guards. I spent a month in St Anne's.

It was revenge for being taken to the hospital against my wishes that I killed Colette. I feel very sick and weak. The shock is getting me. When I killed her I got an experience I will never forget. It is terrible when you realise you have taken a life.

When I caught her outside the house I did not have any wrong or depraved feelings. I just felt that I was suffering a lot due to stress and my mind was unbalanced at that time. When I was standing outside the house I grabbed her because she was the nearest to me. When I stabbed her I knew that she was seriously injured. I flung the knife underneath the floorboards.

I could never kill again and I know this emphatically. If I had got assurance from the 'Mental home' last week it would never have happened. I am a normal man. I had a terrible feeling that I would be locked up for the rest of my life and my mind snapped.

I prayed that night that the little girl would live. I have not slept very well since. I burned the holster for the knife when I got home that night. I am feeling better now that I have told the truth. I could not sleep very well that night. I had nightmares and hallucinations.

The fact that Tobin had mentioned that he had buried the knife under the floorboards of Trampas house was final proof that I had the right man. As was often the case in murder investigations, I did not disclose the full details to the newspapers as unstable suspects could read them and might confess to them. In this particular case, I never revealed that we had found the knife under the floorboards.

Francis Anthony Tobin was born in Cork on 29 September 1948, the youngest in a family of seven. His father left the family around 1960 and never returned. Tobin left school at 14 and worked as a spray painter. In 1968 he went to England, but returned to Cork four years later and was unemployed.

He attended Our Lady's Mental Hospital in Cork as an outpatient, but was admitted on 14 December 1973. He was discharged four weeks later and advised to continue as a twice weekly outpatient. He failed to do so.

He was a single man who lived with his mother and two older brothers, and had never previously been in trouble with the police.

In court he was declared unfit to plead and was detained in the Central Mental Hospital in Dundrum.

I was very impressed by the extent of assistance given by the public in this case. The local gardaí worked very hard to bring the killer to justice. Detective Superintendent D. Dwyer, Chief Superintendent Adrian Culligan, Detective Inspector Tim O'Callaghan and Detective Garda Flan Wiley were to the forefront of this investigation.

However, I found it a very distasteful case. I did not doubt that Anthony Tobin was mad, but he had vented his anger at the authorities i.e. the mental hospital employees, by killing Colette Cronin. My problem with these insane murderers is that they never appear to pick on somebody bigger or stronger than themselves. They always seem to prey on weaker members of society. I have no time for these killers. My sympathy was reserved for Colette Cronin's parents, relations and her two small, terrified friends.

9 'WHY DID YOU DO THIS, SON?'...

JOSEPH JOYCE'S body had 38 stab wounds when it was found on the morning of Sunday, 4 September 1983, the day of the All-Ireland hurling final. Two of the wounds were fatal, one had gone through his heart and another had punctured his left lung.

He was 69, an age at which most people would expect to avoid a violent death, and lived in Westport, Co. Mayo. He had been last seen leaving the Sally O'Brien pub in Peter Street around 11.30 closing the previous night. Seven hours later his brutalised body was discovered in the grounds of the town's Christian Brothers' school on the Newport Road.

It was an unlikely murder setting and an equally unlikely murder victim. Joseph Joyce, it was later to emerge, had paid the ultimate price for being in the wrong place at the wrong time. And that price had been exacted with unprecedented savagery.

Within hours of arriving from Dublin to take charge of the investigation, I knew the type of knife used in the murder. The owner of the West Bar in Bridge Street, Westport had discovered an empty knife-box in the pub toilets that morning. He remarked to his wife at the time that somebody 'had gone out well armed'. When he heard of the murder, he immediately contacted us.

The box carried the description 'Fiton Knife G96 and 920'. A young man had bought a knife of that type in a fishing tackle and sports shop on Bridge St. the day before the murder. The owner described him as between 22 and 25, of slim build, around 5 feet 6 inches tall, with a thin, pear-shaped face. He had ginger brown hair, thick and bushy and neatly kept with a low hairline.

The man had said he wanted to buy a present for his brother. After looking for a fishing reel, he settled on a Tital model knife with a blade five inches long.

At Westport's Central Hotel, the barman remembered a 'strange' looking young man coming in at 10.30 the night before the murder. He sat at the bar, bought a copy of *An Phoblacht* and drank a pint of Harp while he read. As he ordered a second pint, he began looking around as if searching for something. He paid for his drink, then checked through his coat pockets and again looked at the floor. A customer asked if he had lost something, but there was no reply. The customer remarked: 'You never moved from there since you came in, so you could not have lost anything there.' The man finished half of the pint in one mouthful and left the hotel.

The barman's description of him matched that which we had been given earlier.

A number of witnesses eventually provided us with a name for the mystery man. He was Thomas Kirwan from Cortoon, Glenhest, near Westport, who worked at the ESB's plant in Moneypoint. He had been seen on the Glenhest Road on the Sunday and one man said he had given him a lift, dropping him off near his mother's house.

I travelled to Ennis with Detective Sergeant Tony Hickey to check out Mr Kirwan. It was suggested to me that the local Gardaí might do the cross-checking. However, one of the lessons I learned during my career was to always send an investigating team to the area as they have a far greater interest. They also know more about the circumstances. I also visited Limerick and spoke to the local gardaí who knew Kirwan. There we learned that he had been convicted for the arson of a school and a dwelling house and that two women were lucky to escape from the fire with their lives. In November, 1979 he had been sentenced to three years for the house fire and to five years for the school blaze, the sentences to run concurrently. He spent three years and four months behind bars and during that time, was transferred to Limerick Mental Hospital for treatment. He was released in December 1982.

The witnesses from Westport, including the shopkeeper who sold the knife, travelled to Moneypoint for an unusual identity parade. We asked them to point out the man they had seen in the town that weekend from among the labourers working at the ESB station. They all identified Thomas Kirwan.

We picked him up on 21 September at Carrow, Cooraclare, Clare, on a charge of a break-in at a Limerick newsagent's shop some months earlier in which his fingerprints had been found. He admitted the break-in and was then told we were investigating the murder of Joseph Joyce in Westport.

In a confession, which he volunteered almost immediately, he said he had gone to Newport that weekend to visit his mother.

> I am working with McInerney's at Cooraclare. My father got me the job before Christmas. I stay in a rented house there with my father. My father has a house in Limerick.
>
> I have one brother named Francis. My father and mother are separated for a good few years. My mother lives with my grandmother at Cloondaff, Glenhest, near Westport. I go to see her about once a month.
>
> That Friday he had got a series of lifts from Clare to Newport, arriving around 8 p.m. at his mother's house. On Saturday, he had thumbed a lift into Westport.
>
> I had a few drinks in the West Inn. I stayed there for a good while. I walked up the town and I had a few pints in another small pub. I don't know the name of it.
>
> I left there and went into a fishing tackle shop. I was going to buy a fishing reel. I saw a hunting knife in the shop and another one in the window. I told the man in the shop that I wanted to buy the one in the window for my brother. I told this to the man, that it was a present for my brother, in case he would not sell it to me on account of me having drink on me. The knife cost me about £20. There was a black leather scabbard and the shopkeeper put it in a box, then into some kind of paper bag.
>
> I went straight back to the West Inn and had a few more drinks there. It was coming up to 5 p.m. I went into the gents' toilet and left the knife-box there as it had been falling out of my pocket. I put the knife into the pocket of my combat jacket. The knife is in the house in Cooraclare, in my green canvas bag on the floor of my room.

Kirwan told how he had gone from the West Inn to a butchers and bought a few chops, then went back to the West Inn for more drink.

> After a while I decided to go home. I walked out the road. When I did not get a lift, I went back into the West Inn. I went from there to Gibbons' pub. I'd say it was late then.

> I went from there to the Central Hotel. I sat up at the counter in the bar there. I think I had a pint of Harp. I thought I lost money and I had a look around the floor, but didn't find it. I said to someone that I lost £70 or £80.

> From there I went to Gibbons' pub, leaving about closing time. I took a racing bike from just outside the pub and cycled out the Newport Road. But something went wrong with the bike, and I abandoned it. Then I walked back to Westport, about a mile, and took another bike from near Gibbons' pub also. I took this bike as far as the garage opposite the CBS school and walked back into town. I wanted something to eat but I didn't get anything.

> I walked back to where I had left the bike. I met an oldish man. He said something to me. I never saw him until that. I was minding my own business. I cannot remember what he said but it made me very angry.

> I took the knife out of my pocket and I don't remember how many times I hit him with it. I can remember the man staggering and falling down. I kept lashing out at him with the knife. He may have staggered across the road. I had lost the head completely by this stage and I gave him a few more belts.

> I walked out towards Newport and I saw that my hands and the knife were covered in blood. I got a cut in my hand between the thumb and the first finger. I went out the road and over a wall near a house. I slept in a car there. I think it was a Fiat Mirafiori and it was in the driveway of a house.

> I woke up the next morning and went to the garage and got the bike that I had taken from outside Gibbons' pub. I cycled to Newport. I had washed my hands and the knife in a well at a house where there is a 'For Sale' sign up, on the Newport Road out of Westport.

Kirwan then walked through Newport and out the Glenhest Road.

I got into my mother's house at about 10.30 a.m., on Sunday morning. I told my mother and grandmother that I had spent the night with friends in Westport. I went to bed then and got up at about 4 p.m. After getting a bit to eat, I went out for a walk. I came back to Clare on Monday morning with the rest of the gang.

I never washed the clothes I was wearing in Westport that night. The jeans were left into a cleaners in Kilrush by my father yesterday. The rest of the clothes are in a house in Cooraclare.

I am sorry for what I've done. The drink is the cause of all my trouble. I got a fierce shock when I heard the man in Westport was dead. I knew I had stabbed him a few times, but I did not know how bad it was.

Thomas Kirwan's father visited him in the Garda Station in Ennis, where he had made the statement. He sat down next to his son and asked him 'why did you do this?'

His son replied: 'Too much drink.' His father then said: 'You should get yourself examined.'

'It's too late now,' said his son.

At the Central Criminal Court in Dublin on 25 June 1984, Thomas Kirwan pleaded guilty but insane to the charge of murdering Joseph Joyce, the man he met by chance that night on Newport Road. He was committed to the Central Mental Hospital. In October 1995, his case was reviewed by an advisory committee set up by the Minister for Justice and he was transferred from the Central Mental Hospital to hostel accommodation.

10   HERREMA: MY TOUGHEST CASE...

T HE HERREMA kidnap case, fortunately, did not involve murder but it was one of my toughest investigations. First we had to find the hostage. Then it took a 17-day armed siege at a house in Monasterevin, Co. Kildare, the longest in the history of the State, before he was freed and the kidnappers arrested.

It was a tense and testing time, with the drama being played out before the cameras of the world's media. Afterwards we received international praise for the 'softly softly' approach which had resolved a very dangerous confrontation without loss of life.

The praise was welcome and merited. But it had to be seen against the damage done to the country's image abroad through its portrayal as a place where foreign industrialists could be seized by armed gangs and held hostage.

Dutch-born Dr Tiede Herrema, was managing director of Ferenka, a steel-cord factory at Annacotty, Co. Limerick. On 3 October 1975, he had left his home in the Limerick suburb of Monaleen, at 8 a.m. to drive to work. He never arrived.

His car was found abandoned at Monaleen Road, a short distance from his house. Soon afterwards a telephone caller to the Dutch Embassy and the Dublin offices of the *Irish Press* said he had been kidnapped. The caller warned that he would be killed unless three political prisoners, Dr Rose Dugdale, Kevin Mallon and Jim Hyland were released.

A check on Dr Herrema's background showed that he had studied psychology and had a doctorate in the subject, a qualification that could be helpful in his present plight. He had also experienced captivity before — at a prisoner of war camp at Almasford in Holland in the 1940s following the German invasion. The 54-year-old doctor, born in Utrecht, was employed by the AKZO Group, owners of Ferenka, and had moved to Limerick just two years earlier.

The woman caller to the Dutch Embassy had demanded that the three prisoners be freed within 48 hours. She also demanded that the Ferenka factory close down for 24 hours and that no roadblocks be set up by the Gardaí or searches made.

But the searches were soon under way. A number of witnesses who had passed close to the scene of the kidnapping, said they had seen a dark green Cortina driving slowly up Monaleen Road near the Herrema house. One had seen a garda standing at the side of the road close to the Cortina. Some thought they had seen two gardaí in the car.

One woman, a Mrs Moynihan, had a lucky escape that morning. She worked at Ferenka and usually travelled with Dr Herrema. That particular morning she was anxious to avoid going with him because of a strike at the factory. Walking down Monaleen Road, she heard him opening his garage door and starting the car. She hid in a gateway and he drove past and on down the road.

Mrs Moynihan then met a friend and stopped to chat. While the two women were talking, a green car raced past them down the road. Minutes later, Mrs Moynihan passed Dr Herrema's abandoned car.

Witnesses disagreed about how many were in the Cortina. She thought five, others three. Some thought a woman was driving while there was also disagreement about how many men wore Garda uniforms. However, it was easy to piece together what had happened: one or two bogus gardaí had flagged down Dr Herrema. The green Cortina had then pulled alongside and the kidnappers had bungled their victim from one car to the other before speeding away.

At Doon, 14 miles from Limerick City, two garage employees had noticed a green Ford Cortina pull into the forecourt. One of the men filled the tank with £5 of petrol. The garage attendant told us he thought there were five men in the vehicle, and that there was a Z and 9 on the registration plate.

An observant officer, Sergeant J.P. Nolan, filled in another piece of the jigsaw when he stopped a dark green Ford Cortina, registration 8198-Z, near the Parkside Hotel on the North Circular Road in Dublin.

A quick investigation revealed it was a resprayed grey Cortina, which had been stolen earlier from Grange Golf Club in Rathfarnham.

Another witness had spotted the green Cortina in Roscrea, Co. Tipperary, while from Limerick to Dublin on the morning of October 3, the day of the kidnap. In the car, he said, was a woman, sitting in the front passenger seat, a man with a bandage around his head, a man dressed in a Garda uniform and two other men in civilian clothing.

The search for Dr Herrema now intensified to become the largest operation ever mounted in the Republic. I used every resource available, including helicopters. Thousands of miles of terrain and hundreds of derelict and deserted buildings were checked. The kidnappers' demands offered a clue to their identities. We checked the movements of all subversives that could be linked in any way to the kidnapping. We made a connection.

On the 21 October, a Mr Tynan was interviewed in Co. Offaly. Just before the kidnapping, a number of people had stayed overnight in his house. Three of them had arrived in a green car. Mr Tynan said he knew only one of them, a Mr McGowan. There was information from another source. An IRA man, who worked in the Ferenka factory came forward to offer assistance. He had done so he said out of personal admiration for Dr Herrema, his boss. His information proved to be helpful.

One name led to another and so on. We interviewed a Mr Brian McGowan. After we arrested him, he jumped from my car while we were travelling with Detective Inspector Myles Henshaw through Tullamore. We gave chase and managed to arrest him and take him to Tullamore Garda Station.

In a statement he said he agreed to help Eddie Gallagher kidnap Dr Herrema to use as a hostage to free Rose Dugdale. McGowan went to Limerick to monitor Dr Herrema's movements. Later Eddie Gallagher visited him, accompanied by Marian Coyle. He said that two previous attempts had to be aborted.

McGowan's brother-in-law, a Mr Welsh was another accomplice in the crime. McGowan admitted that everyone bar Marian Coyle was armed. He confirmed that Gallagher wore a Garda uniform in the kidnap.

He eventually agreed to accompany detectives to Monasterevin, where he pointed out a house at Kildangan as the one where Dr Herrema was being held. The hostage had been moved from this address by then but those we had arrested let slip a name which provided us with another likely hideout in St Evin's Park, Monasterevin.

It subsequently emerged that Herrema had first been taken to the home of a bachelor farmer in Mountmellick, near Slieve Bloom mountains and kept there overnight. After going to Mass the following morning he bought a newspaper and recognised the picture of Dr Herrema as the stranger being held in his house. He went to a priest and told him to tell the Gardaí about the doctor's whereabouts. However, the priest declined, later claiming that a priest is not obliged to pass on information given in confidence.

Meanwhile, we began checking the police files on Coyle, Gallagher and the mother of his child, Rose Dugdale.

Marian Coyle was born in Derry in 1954, one of a family of 12. She had worked in her father's shop for a time and had no previous convictions. However, the RUC wanted to question her about a bomb planted in a shop in Derry in 1972. She wielded extreme influence over Gallagher, and her determination helped to prolong the siege. A good-looking young woman, her appearance was deceptive. She was capable of unprovoked cruelty and on one occasion savagely bit into the wrist of a garda who was accompanying her.

The other woman, Rose Dugdale, was born in Devon in 1941. Her family were reputed to be wealthy and had sent her finishing school in France and Germany. Later she attended St Anne's College, Oxford, where she obtained a third class BA Degree in politics. She then took up a post with the United Nations as an economics adviser.

She had first come to the attention of the Garda following a spectacular bombing attempt on an RUC station in Strabane. A helicopter had been used to drop two milk churns on the station, but fortunately they did not explode.

Amongst the suspects was Eddie Gallagher, a well known local republican, who had been in England for a number of years. He was now associating with a mystery Englishwoman who was scruffily dressed and with dirty fingernails, but with a posh accent and with a very intriguing habit of ordering two drinks at one time. She was called, it emerged, Rose Dugdale, and a complete description of her was circulated to all Garda stations.

After her UN stint she turned to crime. In 1973 she helped rob her family home of £80,000 worth of paintings. She was convicted and given a two-year suspended sentence. A year later, she was convicted and sentenced to nine years in prison for receiving stolen goods — the Beit paintings.

Gallagher, a native of Donegal, was born in 1948. He had met Dugdale in 1972, the same year he was arrested in Donegal Town for possession of explosives. He was found guilty and sentenced to four months in prison. Two years later, he was back in Portlaoise Prison, remanded on a charge of possessing a firearm and a detonator. He escaped with 18 other prisoners and had never been recaptured.

Family circumstances may have contributed to his involvement in crime. His mother died when he was just 12 years old, which proved to be an emotional trauma for a young boy.

We now had the address where the kidnappers were holding Dr Herrema. About 10 suspects had been interviewed, but some of them were not directly involved in the crime. They knew what happened and the location of some of the safe houses but had not committed a crime. Some of them had been threatened with death if they gave information to the Gardaí.

On 14 October, we had actually searched the house in St Evin's Park, Monasterevin Park, where we now knew Dr Herrema was being kept prisoner, but had missed him. A Mrs Lucy Hall had admitted the gardaí on that occasion and they had searched every room except the attic, where the kidnappers were hiding. It was probably just as well. If Gallagher and Coyle had been discovered, Dr Herrema would probably have been shot.

Afterwards, Mrs Hall said that if the Gardaí had attempted to gain access to the attic, she would have warned them. She told one garda who was involved in the search: 'We are two lucky people that we are not in two wooden boxes'.

The siege at the house started on 21 October. Gardaí, backed up by Army snipers, surrounded the building. Detective Superintendent Ned O'Dea announced their presence through a loudhailer. 'Gallagher, this is the Gardaí' he shouted. 'The house is surrounded by the army and the Gardaí. Come down with your hands up'.

Gallagher replied by firing a shot from upstairs and a piece of plaster fell at the feet of the Superintendent. Then Eddie Gallagher shouted his defiance: 'Fuck off, you cowards. Come up and get me. If you come up the stairs, I will blow the fucking head off this fucking Dutchman.' He followed that with a shot through a bedroom window over the front door.

We then heard Dr Herrema's voice for the first time. He pleaded: 'Please stay away. Tell the police to stay away. Do not come into the house or he will shoot me. He has a gun to my head.'

Superintendent O'Dea continued to call on Gallagher to surrender. Gallagher continued to shout verbal abuse and fired four more shots through the window. Further appeals from the Superintendent led to another warning from Dr Herrema. 'Tell the police to stay away,' he shouted. 'Do not come nearer. They have a gun to my head. They have me wired with explosives.'

A stalemate began that was to last for 17 days. Food and drink was provided to the kidnappers and the hostage while negotiations went on. The food was pulled up from the hallway by means of a rope tied to a basket.

On Sunday 26 October, we tried something different. Detective Inspectors Myles Hawkshaw and John Murphy removed tiles from the roof in an effort to get into the house. They managed to make a hole into the attic, but as they were replacing the tiles, a shot rang out and they felt the bullet hit the roof beneath them. A bullet had travelled through the plasterboard walls of the bedroom and an adjacent bedroom and into the attic.

On Friday 31 October, we tried again. Detective Inspector Murphy and Detective Sergeant John Egan climbed up two ladders at the back of the house and began to remove the putty holding the bathroom windowpane in place. Suddenly there was a gunshot from inside the house, and a bullet shattered Sergeant Egan's index finger. He managed to scramble down the ladder and was taken by ambulance to Portlaoise Hospital, where the finger had to be amputated.

The siege finally ended on the night of 7 November. At 8.30 p.m. Marian Coyle asked for a doctor to treat their hostage. He had a sore neck, she said, and asked for deep heat ointment. Superintendent O'Dea refused.

Half an hour later, Herrema asked to speak to the Superintendent. He said that all three of them were coming down and asked that a doctor be available to treat his injury.

Superintendent O'Dea insisted that all the guns must be thrown out the bedroom window and that Dr Herrema come out of the house first. At 9.30, all three of the guns were thrown out. Then Dr Herrema came down the stairs, followed by Gallagher and Coyle, who were driven away to the Bridewell in Dublin.

The case received worldwide media coverage, portraying Ireland in the worst possible light. At the same time, the way we handled the case received widespread praise at home and abroad. Our 'softly softly' approach was exactly the right way to deal with the tense and dangerous situation. Dr Herrema had been freed unharmed and that was our main objective.

Among the many interviews I did at the time was one for a Dutch television channel. I tried to paint a better picture of my country and to impress on them that kidnappings of industrialists and businessmen, indeed kidnappings of any type, were extremely rare in Ireland.

I had a number of meetings with Dr Herrema following his release and found him to be a man of great dignity.

Gallagher and Coyle were found guilty at their trial some months later in the Special Criminal Court and were given lengthy prison sentences.

11 FALSE TIP-OFF THAT KILLED BILLY FOX...

THE MURDER of Senator Billy Fox in the Republic in 1974, at the height of the Northern violence, shook the Coalition Government of the day. Mr Fox was a respected member of the Oireachtas and had been a Fine Gael TD for Monaghan. He was also a Protestant.

The fear in Government circles was that his killing could signal the start of terrorist attacks on public representatives.

In fact, as the subsequent murder investigation established, the tragic events of that night happened because of false information. The senator was shot dead when he interrupted a raid on a Protestant farmhouse in Co. Monaghan, the home of his girlfriend. The raiders had been tipped off that guns for the loyalist paramilitary group, the Ulster Volunteer Force, were in the house.

The information was wrong, and tragically, was given by a local family out of pure spite against the Coulsons. The family had nothing to do with guns or paramilitaries — they were totally innocent, respected and law-abiding. The tip-off that was incorrect cost Senator Fox his life and created a nightmare of terror for the family.

It was motorist Thomas McNulty who first raised the alarm. On the night of 11 March 1974, he was driving through Scotstown in the direction of Clones, Co. Monaghan, when he came upon a scene of chaos and destruction. A farm house and mobile home were ablaze and two men and two women were standing dazed and shaken in the yard. One of the men had his hands tied behind his back. He freed the man and alerted the fire brigade. The man told him: 'We have been raided and the house is burning, there is also a man missing and he might have been shot.'

Gardaí identified the people whose house was burning as the Coulson family, a respected Protestant family in the area. Marjorie Coulson, whose mother was the headmistress of the local Protestant school, told them that her boyfriend, Senator Fox, was missing and that his car was abandoned down the laneway to the farm. Next morning, as the search continued, the Senator's body was discovered. He was lying face down in a field, with a gunshot wound to his chest and foot. His body was taken to the morgue at Monaghan County Hospital as the murder hunt got under way.

The Coulson family described the attack to us and said that the raiders seemed to be searching their home for firearms. Senator Fox had arrived while the gang were searching the farm.

Two local men, George McDermott and Sean McGettigan, were arrested just hours after the raid — gardaí had spotted them walking across a road near Clones. Their shoes and trousers were muddy and both appeared nervous. They were detained under Section 30 of the Offences Against the State Act and brought to Clones Garda Station.

I interviewed McDermott on 12 March. He told me that before his arrest, he had been hunting rabbits with a ferret in the fields, something I had often done myself when growing up in Kerry. I knew that you did not hunt at night without a lamp or a net. He lied about using a torch, and then about 'doing a job on the Border'.

Finally, he admitted being involved in the raid at the Coulson family home. It was our first break in the investigation.

When Sean McGettigan was confronted with McDermott's statement, he made one, too. The information received from these two suspects led to the arrest of three other men, Shean Kinsella, Michael Kinsella and James Francis McPhillips.

As a result of all statements, we were able to piece together what occurred that fatal night. It transpired that the raid and murder had arisen from a misunderstanding. An informant of the raiders had heard that a package was being delivered to the Coulson family from Belfast. This informant believed the box contained weapons for the UVF in Northern Ireland.

A raid was organised immediately. Those involved reached the Coulson farm by different routes. An unidentified man handed Michael

Kinsella a .25 pistol with a full magazine. He put a round in the breach. Shean Kinsella got an Armalite rifle and Sean McGettigan took a Garand rifle. James Francis McPhillips got a .45 revolver and George McDermott a .38 pistol. Guns were handed out to three or four other unidentified men.

Robert Coulson was lying on a couch watching television in his mobile home, beside the family farmhouse when the raiders struck. He and his wife had just finished their supper when he noticed a man opening the door. 'Stay where you are and put your hands up,' the stranger shouted at them. Another man entered their home.

Their children, in another room, began crying, but the second man trained a machine gun on Robert Coulson's wife and told her not to move. 'It's guns we are after. You have an arsenal of guns,' he shouted. The raiders tied Mr Coulson's hands together and then marched him outside. A gun was put to his neck and he heard the weapon click, as if being cocked.

He was told to walk to the farmhouse front door and to ring the bell. The terrified prisoner watched as his 75-year-old father opened the door. 'What is happening,' his father asked as the intruders pushed both men back into the living-room where Mrs Coulson and her daughter, Marjorie, were sitting.

A raider switched the light on and off six times and the sound of men's footsteps reached them from the yard. The masked men searched the house twice. Robert Coulson's wife and two children were brought into the living-room. She carried her baby and asked one of the men if she could stand near the fire as the child was very cold. He allowed this, but trained a machine gun on her.

Then, the family nightmare took another terrible twist. Both the captives and terrorists heard a car approaching the house. Marjorie Coulson whispered to her mother: 'I'm afraid that is Billy', meaning Senator Fox, her boyfriend.

It was indeed Senator Fox. He had been courting Marjorie Coulson for some years. Michael Kinsella and two unidentified men armed with rifles told the surprised man to get out of the vehicle.

When the Senator emerged from the car, he suddenly hit one of the unidentified men (according to Michael Kinsella) and ran off in the direction of the farmhouse. A rifleman fired at him but missed. Then

65

some more shots rang out in the dark lane. One of the unidentified men told Michael Kinsella that the man was dead.

For the Coulson family the nightmare was still not over. Now that the raiders had murdered the Senator, they decided to erase all evidence in the mobile house and the farmhouse that might enable the Gardaí to track them down. They wiped various items which they thought they might have touched in the house, so as to remove fingerprints. But eventually their leader decided that arson was the best method of destroying clues.

The Coulson family were moved from the house at gunpoint. Marjorie Coulson guessed there were 12 men involved at this stage, but could not be certain. The raiders then set fire to both buildings and disappeared as quickly as they had arrived.

For Marjorie Coulson, there was now a new ordeal — concern over the fate of her boyfriend. His car was still there, with the key in the ignition, but he was nowhere to be seen. She prayed he was not injured, but in vain. The following Tuesday she had to identify his body at Monaghan Morgue.

We had in custody five of the men who committed these horrible crimes. Sean McGettigan still had the remnants of a stocking mask around his throat when he was arrested. He tried to destroy it in the Garda station and soon afterwards tried to tear up his statement. All the suspects made statements and they matched the Coulson family's account of events.

The five men, Michael Kinsella, Shean Kinsella, Sean McGettigan, James McPhillips and George McDermott went on trial in the Special Criminal Court on 20 May 1974. The trial lasted until 7 June when all five were found guilty of the murder of Senator Fox and sentenced to penal servitude for life. They were also found guilty of setting fire to the Coulson farmhouse and mobile home and sentenced to 10 years penal servitude on each charge. There was a further five-year sentence for possessing firearms with intent to endanger life and two years for having firearms without a certificate. All the sentences were concurrent with the life terms.

This was a very serious crime. Not alone was it an attack on a well respected and law-abiding Protestant family, it was also involved the murder of a respected Protestant Senator, who had been a Fine Gael TD in Co. Monaghan for a number of years. The killing, and the way it happened, caused a heightening of sectarian feelings in the border area. I did my best to cool the temperature. Representatives of the Protestant community from across the border were among the many people who came to offer their sympathy and to express support. I made the point of telling them that we were equally appalled on this side of the Border and that we were determined to bring the perpetrators to justice.

During the investigation I was very impressed by the Coulson family, and particularly by the way they conducted themselves during the trial. Later I discovered that the package delivered to the family home, which had set off the raid and led to the murder, contained knitting wool.

Within a short period of being imprisoned, Shean Kinsella and Sean McGettigan escaped from the Curragh hospital where they had feigned illness. Kinsella was subsequently arrested in Liverpool and given 30 years for the shooting of a policeman. McGettigan was arrested in Granard when he emerged armed with two guns from a house that had been surrounded by gardaí. He has since been released.

12 THE NORTHERN TROUBLES COME SOUTH...

IT STARTED with a bank robbery in Co. Kilkenny and ended in the murder of a popular Detective Garda, a former All-Ireland hurler and a father of four children.

A key factor in this case was the overspill of violence from the Troubles in the North, which had become a source of growing concern to the authorities here. More guns had suddenly become available and there was a dramatic increase in bank robberies.

As the situation deteriorated, it was felt necessary to arm more members of the Force with pistols and Uzi machine guns. We had to fight fire with fire.

Almost two decades after the death of Detective Garda James Quaid, precious little seems to have changed. Members of the Garda are still being gunned down by those who would claim to have a political motivation for their crimes.

The robbery had happened at Callan, Co. Kilkenny, on 13 October 1980. Five men wearing balaclava masks and armed with revolvers and an Armalite had burst into the Bank of Ireland branch there and forced terrified staff to hand over £9,000 at gunpoint. They then drove off in a red Ford Escort, fitted with false number plates, and were last seen heading towards Tipperary.

That night, two detectives were sent to Ballyconnick, Co. Wexford, some 40 miles from Callan, to interview a suspect. Detectives James Quaid and Donal Lyttleton wanted to question Peter Rodgers about his whereabouts at the time of the robbery, but there was no response when they called to his mobile home at Knocktown, Duncormick.

As they were returning to the station, they spotted Rodgers in a blue transit van going towards his home, and turned their car around and followed him. He refused to stop and the country road was too narrow to overtake him. The chase lasted for a mile before the van finally halted. As the detectives approached, carrying torches, Rodgers stood by the van and allowed them to search it.

However, while their backs were turned, he produced a pistol, ordered them out of the vehicle and made them walk at gunpoint to a nearby quarry.

Detective Lyttleton was unarmed. While driving the patrol car he had removed his pistol because it felt uncomfortable and had left it in the car. His partner, James Quaid, had a gun, but with the suspect watching him closely, he had no option but to keep walking.

What happened next is somewhat unclear. Detective Lyttleton said later:

> Rodgers was swinging his gun from one to the other, covering both of us. I did not move and I said: 'Peter, don't do anything foolish'. I really felt that he was going to kill us both down in the quarry. He then kicked me on the left thigh and he shouted: 'Get the fuck down there.'
>
> I still did not go down into the quarry, but I backed away from him, parallel to the road. Detective Quaid was somewhere to the left of me, between me and the quarry. He said: 'Donal talk to him, he is a friend of yours'.
>
> I told Rodgers that whatever he had done was not that serious and to put the gun down. He shouted at me to move and kicked me again in the left thigh. I backed away a couple of paces and I said: 'Surely to God you are not going to shoot us?' He came towards me and I stepped back. As I did so I said: 'Peter stop it, this won't help matters'. He shouted at me to get over there and fired a shot over my head. I saw the flash of the gun. I backed away from him, half stumbling.

As I did, I saw him turn to his right and he shouted something. I thought he was shouting at Detective Quaid. I don't know what he said. I was still running and crouching to my right, when there were two or three shots in quick succession. I heard a groan from Detective Quaid. I had run three or four paces at this stage. I heard Rodgers running after me and I heard several more shots. I don't know how many. I kept running, zig-zagging as I went. I ran about a hundred yards and I got in through a ditch on my right and I lay in it.

After a few seconds, I heard Rodgers' van drive away in the Bridgetown direction. I waited in the ditch and just as I was about to get out on to the road, I heard a sound of a vehicle coming from the Bridgetown direction. I thought it was Rodgers coming back to look for me and I got into the field. I lay there until the vehicle passed.

When the alarm was raised, road-blocks were quickly set up and bulletins were issued to surrounding stations to arrest Rodgers.

Detective Quaid lay dead near the quarry. He had been killed by a single gunshot wound to his lower abdomen. Peter Rodgers' version of what happened was given to Edward Wheeler, a noted Wexford hurler, who innocently gave him shelter that night. 'We were chatting at the van,' said Rodgers, 'and I said to the lads it was time to go for a pint. The two lads searched the van and I went to the front of the van and got a gun. The lads found some stuff in the van and I pleaded with them for 20 minutes to let me go and that the stuff was to be used in Northern Ireland, and not in the South.'

Rodgers claimed that Detective Lyttleton flashed a light in his face and said he saw him shielding the other man. He fired a shot over their heads and pleaded with them to let him go. A bullet zipped by his head, he alleged, and he fired at the gun flash. As he got into the van, another bullet whizzed past him, he told Edward Wheeler.

The hunt for Rodgers did not last long as he surrendered to the Gardaí at Wexford the day after the murder. It emerged that following the shooting he had abandoned his van at the home of a Raymond Kelly in Wexford and taken a car from there. He was armed with a revolver and limping from a foot wound. The car was later abandoned at Whiterock View, a local housing estate in Wexford Town and he stayed the night there with Edward Wheeler, who believed his story that he

Garda divers searching for the wreckage of Lord Mountbatten's boat.

Bringing the engine of Lord Mountbatten's boat ashore.

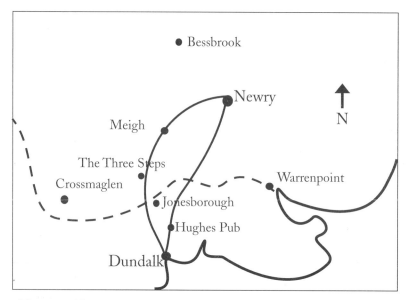

The area of South Armagh/North Louth where Captain Nairac was killed.

*Liam Townson, a member of the
IRA, who was tried for the
murder of Captain Nairac.*

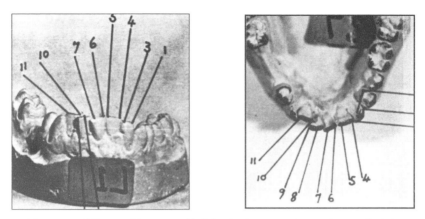

Bite marks: The moulds taken of Michael Flynn's teeth exactly matched the marks on Denise Flanagan's body

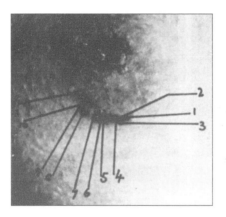

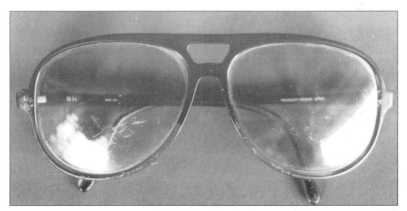

Vital Evidence: Michael Flynn's glasses which were left at the scene of the crime.

The house in Togher where Colette Cronin was stabbed by Anthony Tobin.

Colette Cronin's friend talking to a garda about the incident.

Colette Cronin's friend at the scene of the crime in Togher.

*Dr Tiede Herrema, the Dutch
businessman who was kidnapped
in Limerick in 1975.*

*The fishing shop in Mayo where Thomas Kirwan bought the knife that was to
become a murder weapon.*

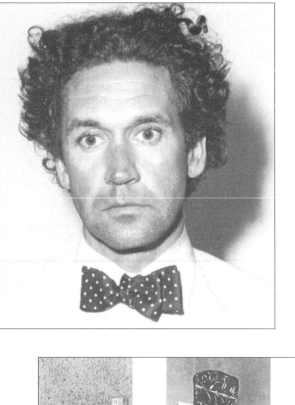

Malcom McArthur, the killer of Nurse Bridie Gargan.

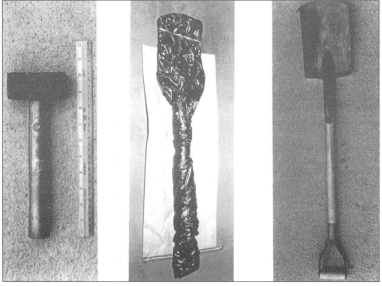

The murder weapons under scrutiny at Garda Headquarters.

Nurse Bridie Gargan who was battered to death.

Crime Scene: The Phoenix Park

Kidnap victim: Don Tidey, the head of the Quinnsworth/Crazy Prices supermarket chain, reunited with his family.

had suffered the injury when he crashed his van. Next day, when he heard of the killing, he persuaded Rodgers to surrender.

At 8 p.m. on Tuesday, 14 October, Rodgers walked into Wexford Garda Station. Asked what he had done with the revolver, he replied that he had thrown it away. I was in the interview room when he asked to see Detective Lyttleton. The two men met face to face, and Rodgers said: 'I am sorry, Donie.' While talking to Detective Lyttleton, Rodgers made some remarks which gave us details as to what actually occurred. I was present at the time and began to take notes although Rodgers was unaware of this. These notes were accepted as evidence at the trial.

The reason for his violent reaction to his van being searched soon became obvious. It contained one Armalite rifle, one sawn-off shotgun, one 9mm Luger pistol, one .45 Colt revolver, assorted ammunition, gelignite, detonators, home-made initiating charges, radio equipment and personal disguises, including wigs.

A doctor who treated Rodgers' injury removed a bullet from his foot. It had been fired by the murdered detective. His pistol was discovered underneath his body with the safety catch off and the magazine empty. This meant that Detective Quaid had fired 25 bullets at Peter Rodgers. Most of the shots that Detective Lyttleton had heard had come from his partner's gun and had forced Rodgers to flee.

Other spent cartridges found at the quarry indicated that in all, more than 30 bullets had been fired at the scene of the murder. Peter Rodgers, who was now facing possible execution if found guilty of the capital offence of murdering a garda, refused to make a statement, despite lengthy questioning. He had been born in Belfast in 1944, had married just three years before the murder and had one child. He had no known criminal convictions but the RUC circulated a memorandum in 1972 naming him as one of the escapees from the Maidstone Prison ship in January of that year.

The murdered officer, Detective Quaid was born on 16 November 1937, in Co. Limerick and joined the force when he was 21. He was transferred to Wexford in 1958 and appointed to the Detective Branch in 1979. He was a popular and highly respected member of both the force and his community. He had been a noted hurler, winning an All-Ireland medal for hurling, with Wexford. The large attendance at his funeral was a measure of the esteem in which he was held. He was survived by his wife, Olive and four children.

At the trial in the Special Criminal Court in Dublin, Rodgers was found guilty of the murder of Detective Quaid. It was a capital offence, but the sentence was subsequently commuted by the President, on the advice of the Government to 40 years penal servitude, with effect from July 1981. He is still in custody.

Like the rest of the force, I found it dismaying to see more and more colleagues being killed in the line of duty. That it is still happening today, 16 years later, demonstrates that we still live in the shadow of the gunman.

13 THE STRANGER IN THE ATTORNEY-GENERAL'S APARTMENT...

QUESTION: WHERE would you least expect to find the man you suspected of being a cold, calculating killer?
Answer: Staying as a house guest in the luxury apartment of the Irish Attorney-General, the State's top legal officer.

Charles Haughey, the then Taoiseach, called the circumstances of the case Grotesque, Unbelievable, Bizarre and Unprecedented — and the sharp-witted Dr Conor Cruise O'Brien immediately coined the term GUBU, which haunted the Haughey administration for the remainder of its term. It has since passed into the general political lexicon as denoting a damaging *faux pas* by those who govern us.

But Mr Haughey's description was particularly apt. This WAS a bizarre and unbelievable case, one which cost the Attorney-General, Patrick Connolly, his job and sent shock waves through the Government. Worst of all, it involved the brutal murders of two innocent people, deliberately singled out by a cold-blooded killer.

The first victim was 25-year-old nurse, Bridie Gargan. On the afternoon of 22 July 1982, while driving through Phoenix Park on her way home to Castleknock from St James's Hospital in Dublin, she decided to stop and sunbathe in the sweltering heat close to the American Ambassador's residence. A gardener there saw her, an attractive, fair-haired girl, relaxing on the grass in the sunshine. He also noticed a man strolling towards her.

The man forced Bridie Gargan into her Renault 5 car at gunpoint. Then he produced a lump hammer and began to beat her savagely about the head and shoulders. The horrified gardener rushed to her assistance.

As he approached, the attacker covered his blood-stained victim with newspapers before pointing a pistol directly at the gardener's head. 'Don't get involved,' he hissed.

Ignoring the threat the brave gardener lunged at him and a brief scuffle ensued before the gunman broke free, leaped into the Renault and drove across the grass towards a jogging track. The gardener rushed to the main road and tried to stop a passing car to raise the alarm.

Nurse Gargan later died from her injuries and a full scale murder hunt began. Her parents, originally from County Mayo, but now living in Dunshaughlin, County Meath, were devastated by the killing and particularly by the brutal manner of her death. She was one of a family of 11, and five brothers carried the coffin at her funeral in the small church at Curragha, near Dunshaughlin. Hundreds of mourners attended. The Renault 5 had been discovered in a laneway off Rialto in Dublin, with the dying nurse in a pool of her own blood in the rear seat. She had been rushed to St Laurence's Hospital and was placed on a life support machine. But it was too late. As I examined the blood-stained car, I blotted the image of the battered girl from my mind. You have to detach yourself from the normal feelings people experience in such circumstances. I was preoccupied with the hunt for the killer.

A shovel, wrapped in a plastic bag, was discovered at the scene of the attack and sent to the Fingerprint Section for analysis. Then a blood-stained pullover was found in Dolphin's Barn, a short distance from where the Renault 5 had been abandoned. Staff at a local travel agency told us how a man in a state of high excitement, had rushed into the premises to ask for directions, then changed his mind and asked them to telephone for a taxi instead to take him to Dun Laoghaire. The man was in such a state that one girl offered him a glass of water. He swallowed it, and then, seeing a bus halt outside the window, rushed from the building and leapt aboard it.

An ambulance driver, one of hundreds interviewed, enabled me to reconstruct the killer's route as he drove from the crime scene. The man driving the Renault 5 had left Phoenix Park through the Islandbridge

Gate and turned left into the heavy traffic. As he did so, the ambulance driver, who was behind, him noticed Bridie Gargan covered in blood on the rear seat. He also spotted a parking permit for St James's Hospital on the nurse's car and mistakingly assumed that the killer was a doctor taking an injured woman there.

The ambulance driver pulled out, signalling to the Renault to follow, and sped through the traffic with sirens blaring. The ambulance and the Renault 5 turned right at Islandbridge, went across the Liffey, and towards the South Circular Road. The ambulance took a left at Kilmainham and turned in at the Hospital gates, still followed closely by the killer. As soon as the Renault 5 was inside the gates, the ambulance drove further on inside the hospital compound. But the murderer now turned the car around and disappeared back through the gates.

I had a good description of the man we wanted from the gardener who struggled with him. From CIE staff we established that he had got off the bus near The Fingal public house in North Dublin. A member of the public who had been drinking in the pub on the day of the attack provided the next piece of the jigsaw. He had come upon a stranger in the gentlemen's toilets shaving off his dark beard with disposable razors. He thought this most peculiar as the toilet had neither a mirror nor hot water. The stranger had a drink and then ordered a taxi from the pub.

We traced the taximan who had taken the suspect to Dun Laoghaire. But there the trail went cold. We issued thousands of questionnaires to the public asking for information and I appeared in all the national newspapers appealing for help. In most of the photographs, I held up a pullover similar to the one which the suspect had discarded in Dolphin's Barn. I pleaded with the public not to shelter the murderer and even though I did not want to spread alarm, I warned that he could kill again. Three days later he did.

The body of Donal Dunne, a young farmer from Monasterboice, Edenderry, County Offaly, was discovered by a family picnicking on a waste bogland near the Rathangan Road. He was lying face down and the left side of his head had been shattered by a shotgun blast.

Some days earlier Mr Dunne had advertised a gun for sale in a newspaper. He had left home with the shotgun on the day of his death, apparently, to show it to a potential purchaser. The would-be buyer had shot him through the head with his own weapon before stealing his car and driving away. The car was later found abandoned in Dublin's Dame Street.

The common pattern in both killings, with the victim's car being stolen, convinced me that the same man was responsible. The descriptions offered by witnesses also had a lot in common.

A stranger had been spotted lurking around Edenderry before the murder of Donal Dunne. The man had purchased a newspaper and a carton of milk from a shop and then he had then walked towards the canal. He sat near the water, staring into space. Some local people were able to provide details of his mannerisms.

One struck a chord. Some time earlier a Dr William Irwin had alerted us about a man acting suspiciously during a clay pigeon shoot in Balheary, Swords, County Dublin. He thought he could be the fugitive we were hunting. A particular mannerism he had noticed was that the man peered over his glasses when speaking. So did the stranger spotted in Edenderry.

I concentrated the investigation in the Dun Laoghaire area to which our suspect had travelled by taxi. Then, on 6 August, came a breakthrough. A Dun Laoghaire newspaper vendor, John Monks, became suspicious about a customer and contacted us. The description of his customer matched Dr Irwin's. Their mannerisms were identical. The man had worn the same type of pullover that we had discovered in Dolphin's Barn and Mr Monks was also able to confirm that his customer had recently shaved off his dark beard.

I was satisfied that this was our prime suspect, and I was delighted with the information. But I was very disappointed when the team of plainclothes men I stationed around Mr Monks' newspaper stall failed to spot him.

Then came another bizarre development. On 4 August, Harry Beiling answered a knock to his front door in Killiney, Co. Dublin, and found a stranger standing there. The man asked his permission to enter the house, which resembles a mock castle, to take photographs of the scenic views from the building. He told Mr Beiling he had attended some of his private parties in the past. There was no reason to disbelieve him and he was allowed in.

Once inside, the stranger suddenly produced a shotgun and demanded the £1,000 in cash from the startled Mr Beiling. The terrified householder convinced him that he did not keep that amount of cash in the house, so the intruder, looking increasingly desperate, demanded he make out a cheque for that amount. But Mr Beiling, taking advantage of a lapse in the man's concentration, slipped through his front door and ran to safety.

I knew instinctively that this was our double murder suspect. My problem was how to find him without attracting any media attention. If the newspapers published information about an intensive search of the area, the suspect would vanish. The team, led by Detective Inspector Noel Conroy, ably assisted by Detective Sergeants Hickey and Donegan, conducted the search with such skill that not one reporter discovered their secret. I kept in touch with the team day and night.

Meanwhile, the Fingerprint Section had established that a print lifted from the plastic bag which was wrapped around the shovel found in the Phoenix Park matched the one taken from a newspaper found near the canal in Edenderry. It was confirmation that Bridie Gargan and Donal Dunne had been killed by the same man.

After the Harry Beiling incident, I ordered a check at all local banks. We discovered that a man, using the name John Eustace, matched the description of our suspect. Giving an address at York Road, Dun Laoghaire, he had opened an account with one bank in July 1982 and had made a withdrawal the following month. I sent some men to the address but it didn't get us anywhere. I hadn't expected that it would.

The name Malcolm McArthur, which was to dominate the headlines for years afterwards, first cropped up on 5 August, two weeks after the Phoenix Park killing.

A sergeant on duty at Dalkey Station took a phonecall from a man of that name. The man said he had called on Harry Beiling the previous day and that he had only being playing a prank on him when he threatened to rob him. He insisted it had been a practical joke and that no harm was intended. He claimed that he had explained everything to Mr Beiling, but finished the call by giving the sergeant a false address.

At this stage the name Malcolm McArthur meant absolutely nothing to me, but I ordered further intensive enquiries in the Killiney area, and the Noel Conroy team began checking out every resident.

Ninety per cent of murder cases are solved by hard slog and attention to detail and this one was no exception. During the house-to-house checks, a woman told the team that on 4 August a stranger called to her house in an agitated state. He claimed there had being an accident and that he urgently needed her car to take the injured party to hospital. As the woman listened to him, she noticed a rifle butt visible under his coat and slammed the door shut in his face.

A Mr Brady added to that information. He told us that he and two friends were driving past the woman's house when they saw a man thumbing a lift. They stopped and told him to get in, dropping him off further down the road in Killiney. He told them he was visiting a friend there. Mr Brady noticed that he wore a cravat.

On 12 August, one of our detectives interviewed a Mr Solomon who lived at Pilot View, Dalkey and gave him a description of the suspect. He asked if there had been any strangers in the area in the recent past. Mr Solomon mentioned that a neighbour of his, Attorney-General Patrick Connolly, had a nephew staying with him. As he described the visitor, one detail jolted the detective's memory. The man wore a cravat.

With Mr Connolly holding the important post of Attorney-General, I wanted to be sure of all my facts before approaching his house. The intruder a the Beiling house had claimed he had attended parties there and Mr Beiling, helpful to the last, provided the name and address of a woman who arranged some of his parties to help us with an identity check.

She confirmed that Malcolm McArthur had indeed attended one of the parties hosted by Mr Beiling in Killiney, but said he was now living in Tenerife. She supplied us with the address of an acquaintance in Mount Merrion, Dublin, who would be able to confirm his whereabouts.

The man confirmed that he knew McArthur and gave the detectives a phone number to contact him. The number was listed as belonging to an apartment in Donnybrook, Dublin, which was in the name of Mr Connolly, the Attorney-General. At the apartment detectives were met by a surprised Malaysian doctor, who said the previous occupants had left some weeks earlier.

The beneficial owner of the Donnybrook apartment was contacted and confirmed that Mr Connolly had lived there until September 1981. After that, a man, woman and child had stayed there until May 1982, when they had emigrated to Tenerife. He also confirmed that the Attorney-General had paid the rent for the duration of the family's stay.

It was time to move in on the Attorney-General's apartment. I was certain that his 'nephew' was the suspect. I ordered a discreet surveillance team to surround the complex and at 4 p.m. on Friday, 13 August 1982, I joined my men. Most of us were armed because we were dealing with a particularly vicious character. At 5.15 p.m. a taxi slowed down outside the apartments. Two of my men questioned the startled driver, who produced two hacksaw blades which he said had been ordered by telephone by a man in No. 6 Pilot View, Dalkey, the Attorney-General's apartment. As we were being told this, a detective spotted a man peering out at us from a window in the apartment. We rushed to the door. I pressed the intercom and made repeated requests to the man to open it. My pleas were ignored.

At this point Mr Connolly arrived home to a nightmarish scene he is unlikely ever to forget. I told him I wanted to interview the man in his apartment in connection with the attempted robbery of Mr Beiling. He was stunned. I did not tell him at that stage of my more serious suspicions about the man. Patrick Connolly, I felt had enough to think about for the present.

The Attorney-General confirmed that the man was not his nephew, but Malcolm McArthur, a friend. The Attorney–General had met McArthur's girlfriend, Brenda Little from Finglas, when she was selling tickets in the city centre. She subsequently introduced him to McArthur. He wanted to try to coax McArthur from the apartment but I would not let him near the door, because the man inside probably had a shotgun. He spoke to McArthur on the intercom, but his appeals to open the door were ignored.

Mr Connolly gave me his keys, but they were of no use as the door was secured on the inside. Then, finally, we heard the voice of Malcolm McArthur. He wanted to speak to his friend, the Attorney-General. Mr Connolly again pleaded with him to open the door and finally we heard the lock being turned. It was a most dangerous situation. McArthur could be waiting inside with a loaded shotgun, ready to blow us apart. Unlike the films, this was a nerve racking scene. One of my team was Detective Francis Hande, who was shot dead some years later while trying to prevent an armed robbery in Drumree, County Meath.

Now, keeping Mr Connolly far away from the door, we drew our weapons and burst into the apartment, expecting the worst. McArthur was standing there. Before he could move, he was wrestled to the floor. Finally, we had our man.

The Attorney-General followed us inside. He told the now handcuffed McArthur that he did not know what was going on, but that whatever it was, he was on his own. He said we could use his living-room to question the suspect and that he was going to his bedroom for a while.

One of my men discovered a shotgun hidden in a storage area underneath the roof of the apartment. I escorted McArthur to the Attorney-General's bedroom and asked Mr Connolly if he owned the gun. He replied that he had never seen it before and was totally unaware of its existence. McArthur admitted that he had brought it to the apartment. I checked the serial number. It was the stolen shotgun of the murdered Donal Dunne.

Mr Connolly said his friend had arrived on 4 August, and that he had agreed to let him stay at the apartment while he settled some financial matters in the country. The Attorney-General listened in shock as I told him that I also suspected McArthur of the murders of Bridie Gargan and Donal Dunne.

He said he would help me in any way he could. I listened as he telephoned Charles Haughey, the Taoiseach, who was in Kerry at the time. I believed that he was completely innocent in the bizarre case which had unfolded, but in my heart I knew his career as Attorney-General was probably finished.

As we hauled Malcolm McArthur from the apartment, he said that if he had known we were coming he would have run away. That came as no surprise.

The whole affair was most embarrassing for the Government as well as ending Mr Connolly's career as Attorney-General. The disturbance in the apartment annoyed some members of the Connolly family. On the night of McArthur's arrest, one family member subjected me to a barrage of criticism for not tipping-off the Attorney-General. When he confronted me in the apartment I explained to him that I was doing my job as a policeman and was not in the business of cosying up to anyone, however elevated their position.

The next day I asked Mr Connolly to make a statement, but he declined, saying he was going on holiday. I explained to him that he was obliged to, and he did, subsequently. True to his word, he did go on holiday, but was called back to Ireland and eventually resigned as Attorney-General.

The story made headlines around the world, while at home the case rocked the Government to its foundations.

On 16 August, while in custody awaiting trial for the murder of Bridie Gargan, McArthur made a full and detailed statement to the Murder Squad.

McArthur, we learned, was an only child of Daniel and Irene McArthur, who farmed at Breenmount a few miles outside Trim, County Meath. He went to England after leaving the local Christian Brothers' School. He also attended Cambridge University, where he graduated with a degree in astro-physics. He returned to Ireland in the early '70s and, at the time of the incident, was 36.

In his statement, McArthur told how he had squandered £70,000 which he had inherited from his father's estate, and was in difficult financial circumstances. He planned a robbery to get some money as he had read about numerous hold-ups in the newspapers since he returned from Tenerife. He bought the shovel to dispose of the body in the event of killing someone during the robbery.

> The first thing was to get the weapon and I went to two clay pigeon shoots, one in Balheary, Swords, County Dublin on 17 July 1982, and the other was in Ashbourne, County Meath on the following day. I want to mention an imitation firearm which I made for myself out of a pistol crossbow which I purchased at Garnet and Keegan after the 8 July 1982. I did not have much faith in this weapon so I cut part of the barrel off to make it look more like a pistol and I built up the top of the barrel with plastic car fillers. I sanded it down to put a fine finish on it and I painted it black. I did this alteration on the pistol while I was staying at a guest house in Upper Georges Street, Dun Laoghaire. I stayed in this guest house because I did not want anybody to know I was in Ireland.
>
> After I came back from Tenerife on 8 July, I started to grow a beard and I purchased a fisherman's hat. Complete with hammer, a shovel wrapped in black plastic, pistol, fisherman's hat and beard I went to these shoots that I mentioned, solely for the purpose of getting a weapon. But I did not succeed.
>
> I remember Thursday 22 July, I left the guest house some time after 2.00 p.m.(carrying and wearing the aforementioned) I got a No 7 or 8 bus into town and I got off the bus on the Quays. I

stood there at the wall for about fifteen minutes admiring two lads who were sitting on two chairs on a barge. It was at the back of my mind that I was now back two weeks and I had not got a weapon to get money. I left the bus terminus and walked along the Quays and up to the Phoenix Park. I entered the park through the Cunningham Road entrance.

I walked along by the Cricket Grounds and I walked parallel to the main road, along the jogger's track, carrying the items. Before I got to the American Ambassador's residence I looked at a few cars but they did not seem easy prey and I walked on. As I walked along the row of trees I saw somebody lying on long grass to the left of these trees and I saw a car parked beside this person. I think the driver's door was open. This car was silver in colour. I walked past the car and I decided to make an approach. I did not know at this stage whether it was a man or woman who was lying beside the car.

I then put my shovel which was, wrapped in black plastic, on the ground beside a tree and I approached this vehicle. As I walked towards the car I had this imitation gun in my right hand and the holdall bag in my left one. When I came within a few feet I saw that it was a lady who was sunbathing. I pointed the gun at her and told her to get into the car. She was very calm and she said 'Is this for real?' And I said: 'Yes it is'. She then calmly said: 'May I put back on my clothes?' I said: 'Yes'. She put a blouse top on. She then got into the back seat of the car. I assured her that I only wanted the car and I told her to lie on the back seat and that I would tie her up. She then began to panic and I panicked because she would not lie on the seat. I was afraid she was going to draw attention to us so I took out the hammer from the bag and I hit her a couple of times because the first blow did not do what I expected it to do. There was blood all over her and some on the window and more on the seats.

I used a newspaper to wipe some of the blood off the left side window. When I was cleaning this window I saw a gentleman walking towards the car. He walked around the front of the car and he said: 'Is this serious?' or something like that. I got out of the car and produced the pistol. I pointed the weapon at him and he stood there for a while and then he ran at me and grabbed the gun. We wrestled for about ten seconds and this man, who was bigger and stronger than me, eventually let me go. If it had been a real gun I may have shot him.

I then jumped into the car and drove off along the dirt track and as I did so, I saw the man out on the main road trying to hail down a car. The girl was moving around on the back seat.

Before I got out on to the main road, by way of the gate which I believe to be the Islandbridge Gate, I passed an ambulance. I arrived at the gate first and the ambulance drove up on my outside. I turned out the gate and turned left and the ambulance again pulled up beside me. The passenger put out his head and said: 'Follow us', or something to that effect. I followed the ambulance and it turned right at Islandbridge and I followed him until the ambulance went into a hospital.

During the time, while I was following the ambulance, I was less desperate but when I turned into the hospital I felt that my need to escape reasserted itself and I wheeled around on the driveway and back out the same way. I think I turned to my left after going out that gate.

I drove towards town. I then got the feeling that I should leave the car and run away. I took a left turn into a narrow laneway and I abandoned the car there. I ran back out the same way and left along South Circular Road. I was still wearing the hat and fawn pullover and I was still carrying the bag. I left the builder's hammer in the Renault 5 and I left the shovel beside where I first saw the girl sunbathing.

As I ran along the South Circular Road I noticed some blood on the front of my crew neck so I took it off along with the hat. I went into a laneway on the left and I left the jumper on some wasteground. I put the hat under some wire. I was getting concerned that the police might catch me and I tried to get on a bus but it did not stop. I then saw the front door of a house open. It had the name 'Odyssey' on it and I walked in. I saw a big pile of leaflets on the floor referring to holidays and I took it then that this was some type of travel agency and I asked the lady if she was an agent for Magicbus. I used this talk to explain and delay my presence. I was panting from the running and she offered me some water. I drank two or three glasses. I then asked her if she could call me a taxi and that I wanted to go to Blackrock. I explained my breathlessness by running on too hot a day in the park to her.

I remained in this premises for three or four minutes and when I left I got on a bus just outside the door. This would have been after 5.30 p.m. I stayed on the bus until it appeared to be getting towards the end. The bus stopped outside a row of three shops and a pub called the Fingal House. I went into a general shop that sold a few chemist items and I bought three disposal razors and I went to the gent's toilet in the Fingal House. I used all three blades and shaved off my beard there. I left two of these blades after me on the floor beside the toilet. I did not use any soap while shaving and it took a long time. When I was in the toilet a number of gentlemen came in and out and one of them spoke to me. When I had finished shaving I went into the lounge and I had a soda water. The barman gave me 5 five pence pieces to use the phone. I rang a taxi and this taxi came pretty quickly. This would have been around 7.00 p.m.

The taxi man was youngish. I asked him to take me to town and when I got there I extended the run to Dun Laoghaire. I had the holdall bag with me all this time. When I got back to the guest house, I noticed that there was some blood on the back of my shirt, so I changed. Later on that day I walked down to the sea near the East Pier and I threw both items of clothing into the sea. Some days later I threw the plastic gun that I used into the sea at Bullock Harbour.

Having obtained a shotgun, McArthur cut 12 inches off the barrel and went to Harry Beiling's house as he thought there would be money there.

I was in his house eight or nine times around 1975 and we were friends then. I pretended that I wanted to take some photographs from his window but instead I produced this gun and I pointed it at him. I demanded £1,000, but he told me that he did not have that kind of money. I then suggested that he could give me a cheque for the money and that a fictitious accomplice, who I told Harry Beiling was working with me, could go to the bank and cash this cheque. I had earlier opened an account in the Allied Irish Bank opposite the Shopping Centre in Dun Laoghaire Village for the amount of £10.00. I opened this account in the name of John Eustace, using a false address at York Road, Dun Laoghaire. I later withdrew £7.00 from this account to give the bank staff the impression that the account was being used.

In my attempt to obtain money from Harry Beiling he made good his escape by running out the front door. I don't know whether I would have shot him or not.

After Harry Beiling had run away from his house, I ran over Killiney Hill. After that I called to another house on the same road and a lady answered the door. I had the gun with me and I wanted her to ring a taxi for me. She told me that her phone was out of order and she did not open the door for me. I then left and a car came along with some people in it who were going fishing and they gave me a lift to Dalkey. I then went to a friend of mine in Pilot View and I have being living there since then. The next morning I brought the gun away and left it under a bush in Merrion Square. I only brought the gun to this address again on Friday 13 August and that is the same gun that I handed over to the Gardaí yesterday.'

McArthur also wrote a note intended for the Taoiseach, Charles Haughey. It read:

Dear Sir,

I have already stated to the police and wish now to state to you also, that my good friend, Mr Patrick Connolly, Attorney, had no knowledge whatsoever of any wrongdoings of mine and must be considered to be utterly blameless. I earnestly hope that the career and happiness of this splendid man shall not be adversely affected.'

Yours sincerely,

Malcolm McArthur.

My boss, Commissioner Patrick McLoughlin, told me we both had to go to Kinsealy to meet Mr Haughey to explain the situation. I gave him the details about the case and he made no comment. Then he poured us each a drink and we talked about his island in Kerry. I was born near Dingle and I remembered when the Blasket Islands were inhabited. I told him something he did not know about islanders — in Dingle we always recognised them because they walked in Indian file. That is because on the islands the only paths are narrow.

Vincent and Bridget Gargan, the parents of Bridie, went on a diocesan pilgrimage to Rome and met the Pope a day before we arrested Malcolm McArthur. Pope John Paul had read about their daughter's death and he told them that he felt deeply distressed and that he would pray for them. He could not believe, he said, that such a terrible thing could happen in the lovely park where he had said Mass. His words were of some comfort to Bridie's parents, though they said they could not put their daughter out of their minds.

I was never in the habit of discussing the work I was doing with my family. However, McArthur's arrest was the subject of much publicity. My wife, Mary, was concerned when I returned home on the day of the arrest and she said, 'What were you up to today? You'll be sacked and who will support the children?' I told her that she had nothing to worry about and that I and the other gardaí on the case had the full support of the family and the justice system.

During his Court appearance, Malcolm McArthur appeared tense and white-faced, and at one stage angry crowds attempted to attack him outside the courthouse.

He pleaded guilty to the murder of Bridie Gargan and was sentenced to life imprisonment in a trial that lasted just 10 minutes, and during which a statement was not read to the court or any evidence given as to what happened. That added to the controversy, as did the State's decision not to proceed against him for the murder of Donal Dunne.

As I write, McArthur is still serving his sentence in Arbour Hill prison. Incongruously, one of the heroes of the investigation, news-vendor John Monks, whose powers of observation helped to put McArthur behind bars, subsequently fell foul of the law himself and appeared in court on theft charges.

In every sense, it was a case which more than merited Mr Haughey's memorable description: Grotesque... Unbelievable... Bizarre... and ... Unprecedented.

14 WHEN A WIFE FINDS LOVE ELSEWHERE...

ANNE BROWNE'S life with her husband John was very unhappy. He spent all their money on drink. In five years he had squandered the bulk of a £63,000 compensation payment, awarded in 1977 following an accident at the ESB Power Station in Tarbert, Co. Kerry, where he worked.

As a result of the injury, he also received a disability allowance of £104 a week. That went the same way — on drink. As he drank more and more, he suffered seizures and became difficult and argumentative, increasing the strain on their domestic life.

To help cope with the problems of a husband she claimed was never sober, Anne sought solace in the arms of a neighbour, Jeremiah O'Sullivan. She was fond of him and he said he loved her. They often discussed how much they would like to live together if her husband — she called him Bob rather than John — 'died in one of the fits he had from time to time'.

Then, just after 1 a.m. on 3 June 1983, John Browne's body was discovered on the road outside Listowel, the apparent victim of a hit-and-run accident. Later, however, a post mortem confirmed that he had been shot twice, in the back and legs.

It was my second murder investigation that week. We had just made an arrest in relation to a murder in Dublin and had travelled to Kerry to join my family, who were on holiday there. Then there came a call from the Gardaí in Listowel requesting that I go to the County Hospital in Tralee to begin an investigation into the murder of John Browne.

We started house-to-house enquiries in the Listowel area but despite intensive checking only one person reported hearing gunshots. Then, suddenly, things began to stir in the sleepy town. The murderer began to feel threatened by the investigation and I knew that the person we were seeking was a local.

One of the first things I did was to revoke all local gun licences and to call in all shotguns for examination. A thorough search of the scene uncovered two empty cartridges.

On 5 and 6 June, in two anonymous calls to Listowel Garda Station, a male caller claimed to have seen a white Capri car close to the murder scene. On 7 June, in similar calls to *The Kerryman* newspaper in Tralee, a man alleged that the IRA were admitting responsibility for the murder, and asked that the Gardaí be told 'there is another man to be knocked off, an informer'.

But the killer's luck had run out. That day, Garda Liam Moloney, from Abbeydorney overheard a phone call being made from a public kiosk in which the word 'informers' was used. As the caller left the kiosk and drove off, he took the number of the car. It was a blue Ford Cortina belonging to Jeremiah O'Sullivan.

O'Sullivan's son owned a shotgun. It was amongst those taken for forensic examination. Someone had interfered with the firing pin of the weapon in an attempt to sabotage the investigation. They almost succeeded but our forensic expert's persistence paid off. He brought the gun to Dublin and finally established that the shotgun belonging to Mr O'Sullivan's son had fired the cartridges found at the scene.

Jeremiah O'Sullivan knew by now that I was on his trail. The breakthrough came when we decided to extend the investigation to Abbeyfeale. The proprietor of Westering Inn recognised O'Sullivan and Anne Browne as regular customers in his pub. He had seen Ms Browne's photograph in *The Kerryman* newspaper and had recognised her. He told us that O'Sullivan had called to the pub on the day following the murder, apparently to establish an alibi, asking if a ring had been found on the previous night, which he claimed his wife had lost.

When he was told no ring had been found, he thanked the owner and walked away, not bothering to leave his address in case the ring was discovered later. That added to my suspicions of him, as did the fact that we subsequently discovered that he had bought cartridges for his gun. I directed that all the members of the family be interviewed at the same time. This was always my strategy for preventing family members from inventing alibis for each other.

Anne Browne's behaviour too had aroused my suspicions when I visited her home. She was very anxious to get on with her husband's funeral. I thought it very strange that she had not looked at any of the Mass cards which were in the house. When I drew her attention to this she said that she hadn't had time to look at them. Mrs Browne was also taken into custody.

We confronted them both with a statement by Mrs Maureen O'Connor of the Westering Inn that neither of them was in the pub on the night of the murder. Finally, eight days after the murder, O'Sullivan confessed. That day, he said, he had taken a load of cattle belonging to the nuns, at the convent in Lixnaw by trailer to the mart in Listowel.

> At about two o'clock, I met John Browne on the street near the phone boxes. I'd say he had a good drop of drink on him. I said 'Hello'. He said: 'Come here boy.' He accused me of taking his wife around. He said: 'If I don't get you tonight, I'll get you tomorrow morning, I'll blow your brains out'.
>
> I got such a fright and such a shock that I sped away from him as fast as I could go. I knew that he was that kind of treacherous guy, that he would shoot me. I went down to my tractor and trailer and I went home. I was thinking about John Browne's threat all evening, and I was certain that he was going to kill me. He was a lot bigger man than me, and naturally enough I was in dread of him. I decided to do something about him. I went to my son's room and took his single barrel shot-gun, and two No. 4 cartridges, from the wardrobe. I put it in the boot of my car, a blue Ford Cortina. I wrapped the gun and cartridges in an old greenish jacket, that could still be in the car.

O'Sullivan told how he had gone to the 7.30 p.m. Mass in Listowel as it was a Holy Day. Later he went to the Square and met Anne Browne.

She is John Browne's wife and I have been going around with her for a couple of years. We often met in the same place. We got into my car and I drove to Thour Creamery, that's on the way to Abbeyfeale, just off the Cork line. I parked in the creamery yard, and we stayed there until about the half eleven mark. I never said anything to her about her husband threatening me that day.

After dropping her off near her home, I drove to Listowel and bought a carton of chips. On the way back to the car, I saw John Browne. He was walking towards home. When I had eaten the chips, I drove on out through Greenville, and I passed out John Browne. I think he was on the Listowel side of Markey's bridge. He was on the right hand side. I drove on and parked in the yard at Scartleigh Creamery. I got the gun out of the boot and put one cartridge into it. I put the other one into my pocket, I waited there for about 10 minutes, it was a fine night and there was a bit of light. I saw John passing the creamery gate and I called him. He was on the far side. I stepped out on to the road, and said: 'Hi John, come here, I want you, boy.' I said: 'Are you as good a man as you were today?' He didn't say anything. He recognised me and he started to run.

I ran after him and fired a shot at him. I think it was low. He kept running, so I took out the used cartridge, and put the other one in the gun. I ran after him and fired the other one. It was darker out there because there were trees. I don't know where I hit him, but I think it was higher than the first shot. I took out the second used cartridge and threw it away. The two cartridges that I fired must be along there somewhere. I ran back to my car, and drove off home. I put the gun in the boot again. I passed by John Browne lying on my right hand side of the road.'

The next morning I got up at about six o'clock. I went to the shed where the car was parked and got the gun out of the boot. I got a file off the bench and I filed the hammer, or should I call it the striking pin on the gun.

O'Sullivan also admitted making the anonymous calls to the Gardaí and to *The Kerryman*, and added: 'No one knows how sorry I am for what happened.' Anne Browne then admitted making false statements to the Gardaí 'because my boyfriend, Jerry O'Sullivan, told me to tell lies'. She told how they met in the Square in Listowel and drove to a creamery yard off the Cork Line, outside Listowel.

We remained there talking until about 11.30 p.m. and had a kiss and a cuddle. During this time, we discussed my husband, Bob, and I complained to Jerry about Bob's drinking and the money he was spending and Jerry said that is a terror.

Jerry never told me that he had met Bob that day and he did not discuss shooting Bob. We discussed on previous occasions what we would do if Bob found out about us. We agreed that Jerry should shoot Bob before he would shoot any of us. The last time we discussed this was about three weeks ago. I am very fond of Jerry O'Sullivan and we often discussed how we would like to live together. Jerry often told me that he loved me and wanted me for himself. We agreed that it would suit us if Bob died in one of the fits he got from time to time. Jerry feels very sorry for me as I tell him all my troubles and the problems I have with my husband when he is drunk — daily. I always believed Jerry because he does not tell lies. On the night of Thursday 2 June, Jerry drove me home from the creamery yard by Finuge to the Grotto near my home. When I was getting out of the car Jerry said, 'if the Gardaí call to you, tell them you were in the Westering Inn with me tonight and that you got home at ten to twelve'. I asked him why but he just shook his shoulders and a queer look came over his face. I told the Gardaí that story.

Jerry called to my house on Friday night, 3 June, and told me that he had shot my husband. He told me to tell nobody and to say nothing about it and I agreed. I did not know that Jerry was going to shoot my husband on Thursday night.

Jeremiah O'Sullivan was found guilty of the murder of John Browne and sentenced to penal servitude for life in February 1984. He was released in June 1993. There was a sad footnote to the case. The postmortem revealed that John Browne had sustained serious brain damage as a result of his accident at the ESB Power Station. This injury would have explained his seizures and, to some extent, his drinking and his argumentative attitude. He had behaved badly, the pathologist felt, because of his mental condition.

One of the most alarming aspects of the case was the fact that as far as Tralee General Hospital was concerned, John Browne had been an accident victim. Incredibly they failed to notice that the man had been shot in the back, something which was immediately obvious to me.

15 DON TIDEY: KIDNAP AND RESCUE...

MURDER INVESTIGATIONS, however difficult, are usually fairly straightforward affairs. You have a victim and your job is to find the killer. With kidnapping, the issue becomes much more complicated. The time factor is crucial. Now your task is not just to track down the kidnappers but to find them before they murder their hostage.

On 24 November 1983, supermarket chief Donald Tidey was abducted by what we later established was an IRA gang. It set off one of the most intensive searches ever undertaken, culminating in a joint Army–Garda comb-out of a 10-mile area around Ballinamore, Co. Leitrim.

It took us 22 days to find and free Mr Tidey, who had suffered an appalling ordeal, which he graphically describes in this chapter. But the price of the rescue was high — an army private and a trainee garda were shot dead by the kidnap gang during the search of Derrada Wood.

Private P.J. Kelly, from Athlone, was 36 and married, the father of three young boys. Garda Garry Sheehan, from Monaghan, was just 23 and still at Templemore. He was one of a number of Garda recruits who had been drafted in to help with the search. Today his courage and sacrifice are honoured in the Garda Sheehan Memorial Medal, awarded to the best individual recruit graduating from Templemore.

Only one member of the gang served time for their crime in this jurisdiction — and he made the mistake of walking into a Garda station, ostensibly to clear his name, two years after the kidnap. Some of his accomplices, we later established, were subsequently jailed in other countries for different offences.

The kidnappers struck when Mr Tidey, boss of the Quinnsworth and Crazy Prices chain, was driving his Daimler to Dublin Airport to catch a flight to Belfast. He was accompanied by his 13-year-old daughter, Susan, who was being dropped off at her school, Alexandra College, in Milltown. Driving behind, in his own car, was his 19-year-old son, Alastair.

As they approached the junction of Stocking Lane and Woodtown Way, Rathfarnham, they saw a police car facing them with a garda sitting in the car and another standing beside it. When Mr Tidey identified himself, he was ordered out of the Daimler by one garda, who produced a revolver from beneath his uniform.

The other bogus officer raced round to the passenger side and pulled Susan from her seat. He was armed with a sub machine gun. Simultaneously, an armed and masked man approached Alastair and dragged him from his car before throwing him face downwards on to the road. The man viciously kicked Alastair in the head when he tried to see what was happening to his father and sister.

Then two more masked men, armed with sub machine guns, came through hedges and raced towards Alastair's car. They fired some shots into the air. Though he resisted, Mr Tidey was bundled into the rear seat of the fake patrol car while two of the masked men stood guard over his children. Within minutes, the gang had gone, taking with them the Daimler and Alastair's car keys. The two frightened teenagers ran to a nearby house to raise the alarm.

Chief Superintendent Patrick Culligan, the recently retired Commissioner, Detective Superintendent Edward Ryan and I headed the investigation. We got a tip-off about the location of Mr Tidey. Some people may scoff and think by a tip-off I mean someone just phoned and handed us all the details on a plate. It does not work like that. We had to earn the information we received.

We earned it by discovering where the kidnap gang had changed cars, in Celbridge, Co. Kildare, and by tracking down a witness who spotted a car near the scene of the swap which was owned by a known member of the IRA. We interrogated this man, who cracked under pressure and gave us the location of the hostage. He was only involved in the kidnapping in a minor way, so we did not press charges against him. But the location he gave us was far from specific — it was a whole area of countryside around Ballinamore, County Leitrim.

On Saturday, December 10, we drew up a search plan for an area extending over a 10-mile radius, from Ballinamore Town. Checkpoints manned by Gardaí and the Army were set up. The search plan was codenamed 'Santa Claus' and it worked as follows: 10 teams codenamed Rudolph 1 to Rudolph 10 were set up and each day a section of the radius was searched. Each group was led by an uniformed Garda inspector. A radio base, codenamed Echo Base, was set up in Ballinamore Garda Station.

On 16 December Rudolph 5 searched Derradda Wood. In the centre of this wood, a hide made from black polythene plastic, with a floor of hay, was discovered. The wood is two and a half miles from Ballinamore Town and directly north of it. The land is rushy scrub and the area was populated by quiet, unhelpful people. Rudolph 5 consisted of one inspector, one detective sergeant, one uniformed sergeant, three detective gardaí, two uniformed gardaí, 10 recruit gardaí and six soldiers.

The trap was set. The rescue was to end in freedom for Don Tidey, but also in death and injury for some of the Army and Garda searchers.

Recruit Garda Joseph O'Connor, one of those involved, described the scene:

> The wood is about two acres in area with fir trees about 15 ft high and thick undergrowth consisting of briars and gorse bushes, particularly at the edge. I was beating my way through the undergrowth with a metal probe and I was being covered by Private McLaughlin. The gorse and the briars were about 5 feet high and I was unable to make any headway. We retraced our steps and followed Recruit Garda Francis Smith, who had discovered a pathway into the wood.
>
> At this stage, Recruit Garda Francis Smith was about 5 yards in front of us. I heard him talking to Recruit Garda Garry Sheehan, who had approached from the opposite direction. I heard him ask Recruit Garda Sheehan if he had seen a man dressed in combat gear, wearing knee high black boots, to his front. There was immediately a burst of rifle fire from our front. I heard a moan or grunt from the position where Recruit Garda Sheehan had been. There was a pause in the firing and Recruit

Garda Smith joined Private McLaughlin and myself. I told them it was too dangerous to try and get out of the wood and that we should take cover.

We lay on the ground between the trees. There were several bursts of gunfire in front of us.

A man was shouting: 'come out with your hands up'. Private McLaughlin was to my right, aiming his gun into the wood but not firing. I looked behind him and saw a man dressed in a camouflage combat jacket lying on the ground and facing us. He was grey-haired and bearded. He was signalling towards us with his hands and whispering what sounded like 'Tidey —Hostage'.

The Private then covered him with his rifle. I crawled towards this man and searched him for weapons. He told me that he was Donald Tidey and that he was a hostage. I instructed him to follow me as I crawled back to my colleagues. We then decided to leave the wood, with Recruit Garda Smith in the lead followed by Mr Tidey and myself. Private McLaughlin covered us.

On reaching the edge of the wood, we entered a small drain and used it for cover as far as the roadway. We got on to the road and were approached by an armed detective. We told him that we had Mr Tidey and he moved off to the left along the roadway with him.

At this stage there was sporadic gunfire from over the hill. At the back of the wood, I saw a blue Opel motor car come around the bend on my right. Immediately shots were fired from this car in our direction. There was a considerable amount of gunfire, including machine gun fire from the car. We lay down in the drain until the firing from the car and the firing from the security task force men, who were positioned in a gateway, stopped.

Another of the Garda recruits, Francis Smith told how during the search he had spotted a man with a gun in his hand.

I thought he was a soldier from the way he was dressed. He had black footwear up to his knees and wore green army style pants and a green combat jacket. He had a white cloth in one of his hands and appeared to be cleaning the gun. The gun was a long barrelled rifle type, similar to the army rifle.

I then heard Recruit Garda Gareth Sheehan call out to me. I said to him: 'Garry, there is a soldier over to my right, about 10 yards in front of you'. Just then I heard commotion to my right and behind me. I heard Sergeant Liam Wall call for assistance from that area. I got down on the ground. Just at that moment, the firing started in front of me and to my right and behind me. It was bursts of automatic gunfire and there were a few loud bangs. I heard shouts from behind me: 'Get back, get back. Get out of the forest.'

The recruit told how Don Tidey had identified himself to them and warned: 'There are vicious men up there. They have grenades. Follow me.' His advice was rejected. Recruit Garda Smith recalled:

I said 'No. We will go our way'. The man replied: 'You fool. I am Donald Tidey'. He was dressed in camouflage gear and wellington boots. I led the way out of the wood towards the road. Joseph O'Connor took off the man's boots to stop him running away, as we were not sure if he was Donald Tidey or not.

One of the officers wounded in the rescue was Detective Garda Daniel Kellegher. He had been raked with gunfire from the car. He said later:

I had just turned a fraction from my position at the hedge when I felt a pain in my left thigh, instantly followed by a similar, more severe one in my right thigh. I slumped forward to the ground and saw a blue Opel car travelling past me on the road.

There were two long barrelled firearms sticking from the left passenger window. They were firing as they passed. I thought we were all dead and expected to be hit again myself. Detective Sergeant Rice called to me and asked me if I could move. I managed to crawl a little bit towards him, using my left leg to propel me. My right leg was extremely painful and I was unable to use it. Detective Sergeant Rice took the Uzi and pulled me into a gap in the hedge. I was bandaged up and hours later a bullet was removed from my right thigh in Cavan Hospital.

Detective Inspector William Somers told how he had pulled Mr Tidey into a shallow drain for safety as a gunman in the car sprayed the area with bullets. Later the inspector discovered how close he had come to death — there were five different bullet tears in his clothing. It had been a close call too for the hostage. He was given a bullet proof vest and taken to Ballyconnell Garda Station.

Later Mr Tidey was to tell us his story, one of extraordinary courage and resilience in the most terrifying of circumstances. During the kidnap he had been hit heavily across the head with a pistol butt, then had a rib fractured as he was forced on to the car floor. He became car sick during the long journey that followed and the pain from the broken rib was 'excruciating'.

At one stage during the trip, he was hauled from the car, with a hood over his head, and 'propelled with a number of blows and a lot of curses' into what he took to be a van. He recalled the van travelling at great speed, but had no way of estimating how far they travelled.

In a statement he told us:

> After quite some time, the vehicle slowed and pulled into rough ground or a track of some description. I was told to get out and I sensed that I was on farmland of some description. It was here that I was searched and then questioned. During the search the most important document that I had on me was a diary, which helped under the circumstances because clearly they wanted the telephone numbers of people who could be contacted outside of the State, and my diary contained such numbers. The questioning took the form of ascertaining who various people were and their relationship to me and their reliability.
>
> I co-operated with their questioning simply because I had assessed that most of the information in the diary could have been obtained by anybody who wanted to know about these individuals, particularly directors and their locations. After that, I was made comfortable and I was given some wind cover with what I believe was a sort of polythene shield and some hay was put around me to keep out a very cold wind. All questioning took place by people behind me. At no time was anybody actually exposed, but my hood was lifted for me to identify particular pieces of information that they wanted from my diary.
>
> I did not know what to expect at that stage. I was told that I had been kidnapped and that there would be a ransom demand made for me. To that end, they needed information which subsequently they secured from my diary. It was at this point that they told me in no uncertain terms that my life was in my own hands and that if I attempted to do anything hazardous that they would have no hesitation in dealing with me if their operation was put at risk.

Mr Tidey was later put back in the vehicle and driven off again. This trip, he recalls, 'was even more uncomfortable than the previous one'. Then, still hooded, he had to walk across country for half an hour.

> There was clearly a lot of discipline among the group of people that I was with. Conversation was at all times peremptory and limited essentially to one person, and was conducted in whispers. The discipline was illustrated by the fact, for example, that nobody smoked and there was no idle chatter. I sensed that the people around me considered this was a serious business. I was under no illusion that my part in the scenario was to maintain the same discipline that had been established. From that point, if I had to converse, it was in a very low whisper.

When they arrived at 'the hide' in Derrada Wood his legs were chained and his hands manacled.

> My hood was removed and an effective blindfold and additional headpiece, which made hearing and seeing impossible, was applied. I was never certain how many people occupied the location, but there was some benefit in us being close because I was secured to one of the people and, secondly, we obtained some body heat from each other in conditions that were particularly difficult.
>
> Most mornings I got tea and bread with some type of filling, normally jam, and that would be eaten either inside or outside the hide, depending on the weather conditions. I was always located in the same spot and chained to a tree. In the late evenings, we visited the latrines located in another area in close proximity. During my sojourn by the tree, the passing of time was marked by the appearance of food, which could vary from hot to cold and from soup to sandwiches.
>
> Early evening was marked by tea, which was either hot or cold, and a substantial meal or a meagre one. This was effectively the last meal of the day before retiring into the hide early in the evening. The question of needing to relieve oneself during the course of the very long hours became a very serious and tedious business. This was due to my confinement in the sleeping bag, the chains, the padlocks and my fractured rib, which made movement within an area of which I had no understanding exceedingly difficult.

He described the routine:

> With eating, the main discipline was to make sure that I had left no residual evidence around me to show that I had in fact been eating there. Food dropped on the floor and that sort of thing was very quickly a source of discipline. On occasions that I had food that was wrapped, i.e. chocolate or a sweet, great account was taken that the paper was handed back.

> For moving to ablutions and latrines I was unchained at the feet, with the halter rope being retained at all times at my knees. It was a question of moving from my stationary position to the ablution or latrines by holding firmly to the rear of an individual and crouching very low because we appeared to be in a very densely wooded and foliaged area. As far as the ablutions went, it involved stripping to the waist and initially being scrubbed, but this I eventually did myself.

> There was a limited amount of water and soap, but I was encouraged to cleanse myself very thoroughly, which I did. There was no question of shaving. I did on occasion have what I believe was a communal toothbrush and toothpaste, which we used sparingly. I managed to arrange that, after a couple of days, I could remove my headgear and this afforded me the opportunity of washing my face and head. But this was only done under very close observation by one or more people and I needed to exaggerate the fact that for the brief time I was washing my head, my eyes were tightly closed.

> As far as the latrines were concerned, the discipline was quite simple in that it meant faeces were deposited on paper, presumably newspaper, and this was collected and as far as I understand removed from the site.

Despite being chained, Mr Tidey managed to develop his own exercise system, 'a modified form of running on the spot which helped my circulation and kept my general physique toned up. Actually, in that position over those hours and days, I probably reached a level of physical fitness that I would not achieve in my normal daily routine.'

There was little communication with his kidnappers. At one stage his hood was removed, he was handed a newspaper and told 'to look cheerful and alive', while his picture was taken with a polaroid camera. 'I think the most significant thing that I attributed to that moment was that for the first time I felt optimism that I was not lost or forgotten. The importance of that statement is that it did give me heart to hold on through what, in the event, turned out to be an extremely long period.'

He measured time from Sunday to Sunday, the routine interrupted only by a change of clothing.

> I was given a fresh pair of socks and wellingtons. A week or so later, I was furnished with a replacement shirt, which was thicker and gave me a good deal more warmth than the cotton shirt I was wearing. On the Monday or so of the week I was rescued, I requested a change of underclothing and indeed a wash of the lower half of my body, because by then I had been in that condition for 17 or 18 days. This I was allowed to do and I was furnished with a pair of briefs.

Then a new problem developed. Mr Tidey had a history of serious ear infections, now aggravated by the water he was using to wash. He told his kidnappers that without ear-drops he would experience severe inflammation and become a liability to them. 'In the event, it took them 48 hours to produce the ear-drops. The routine ear-drops that they produced would not have been sufficient to cope with my situation if I had been in captivity any longer.'

On the day of the rescue, he was warned to keep absolutely quiet as the security forces were about to pass within yards of the hide. His chains and hood were removed and he was given a balaclava which was reversed so that he could not see. As the searchers got nearer, he was ordered to reverse the balaclava, move out of the hide, and follow behind the leader of the section.

Suddenly shooting broke out, he said. 'The gun battle raged around me at this stage. Within a short space of time, I heard somebody cry out. Naturally I thought somebody had been hit and shortly after that there was a violent explosion very close to me.' Mr Tidey then told how in the confusion he had come close to being shot by those who rescued him.

> As I looked around, I saw that within ten feet a soldier had his automatic rifle trained on me. Now I was wearing a balaclava and camouflage outfit and it must be remembered that I did not know whether I was looking at a terrorist or a member of the security forces. Equally, he did not know whether he was looking at one or the other. And so there was a moment in time when we were taking each other in and I had to indicate somehow that I was the hostage.

Once or twice, the soldier came perilously close to firing at me but then, looking beyond him, I saw two gardaí. The soldier motioned one of the gardaí around while keeping me covered. They were still highly suspicious of me and apprehensive, as they quickly searched me. We made our way through some very uneven ground, belly-crawling under the trees, causing my clothes to become tangled. My wellington boots and trousers were removed at that point because it was the fastest way of allowing me to move more freely. We then advanced further, barefoot in my case, across some very broken land and ditches until we came to the road, where I managed to convince Sergeant Rice that I was in fact the hostage.

That Mr Tidey had survived to tell his story meant the main aim of the rescue operation had been achieved, but at a terrible cost. In the confusion the vicious band of kidnappers escaped, but the hunt for them went on. We were determined to ensure the sacrifices made were not in vain.

We discovered that before Mr Tidey's car was stopped at the beginning of the kidnap, the gang had mistakenly thought that a businessman, who lived next door to him and who was travelling on the same road, was their target. They let this man go, but he had noticed that the 'Patrol car' they used had Limerick number plates. He knew all patrol squad cars in Ireland have Dublin registration plates and as his suspicions were aroused, he carefully noted the kidnappers' appearances. He assured us afterwards that he would recognise these men if he ever saw them again. I was very impressed by his courage in offering to do so.

With his help, we established from our files that one of those involved was a Michael Burke, who was a well known member of the provisional IRA from Cork City who had disappeared. Then, two years later, the same Michael Burke walked into Tralee Garda Station and innocently enquired whether the Gardaí were looking for him in connection with a crime, and if so, why. It was a foolish bluff by the man. In the two years that had passed we had not relaxed our investigation.

The businessman who claimed he could identify the kidnappers agreed to accompany us to Tralee. We held an identity parade and the businessman insisted that all the men in the parade should wear Garda hats. We supplied the hats and to our delight, the businessman identified Burke as one of the kidnappers.

It had been an ordeal for the businessman, both at the identity parade and later at the trial, when he was subjected to cross-examination by defence counsel Seamus Sorohan. At one stage counsel suggested that the witness had been cossetted by the Gardaí in Tralee so that he could help acheive a conviction.

At last we had captured one of the terrorists. Burke was subsequently found guilty of the kidnapping and sentenced to 12 years imprisonment in June 1985. Some of his accomplices were later tried in other countries for different offences and jailed. We had identified them from the fingerprints found in the bunker in Derrada Wood.

Michael Burke was released in June 1994.

16 A DATE THAT ENDED IN DEATH...

DEBORAH ROBINSON, the 20-year-old daughter of a Belfast engineer, had travelled south to meet a man who contacted her through a dating agency. She spent some time with him in Swords, Co. Dublin, where he lived — then waved goodbye and left to catch her bus back to Belfast.

She never made it. A chance encounter with a stranger in Dublin ended in her rape and murder, with her body dumped in a ditch in Co. Kildare. It was a difficult case and took us 15 months to crack. Once again, it was the skill of the forensic scientists, allied to the hard slog of routine police work, which finally put her killer in the dock.

It was farmer Christopher Walsh and his daughter who found the body. As they drove their sheep along a side road near Clane, Co. Kildare, on 8 September 1980, one of the lambs jumped a ditch and fell eight feet into the bed of a drainage scheme, where the murdered woman lay. She was dressed in a yellow T-shirt and jeans and State Pathologist Dr John Harbison established that she had been strangled and also sexually assaulted. She had suffered injuries to her head, face and arm while trying to defend herself.

We eventually identified the body as that of Deborah Robinson, from Upper Malone Road, Belfast, whose father had reported her missing to the RUC the previous day when she failed to return home from a day-trip to Dublin. She lived at home with her mother, a doctor, and her father, an engineer, and worked in a textile factory.

The pathologist established that she had been killed elsewhere, then moved to the place where her body was found. She had travelled from Belfast by bus, we discovered, and had got off in Swords, Co. Dublin. The driver said he told her he would be leaving from Parnell Square in Dublin at 6.30 that evening, but she did not turn up.

Then came an unexpected development. Edmund Law, son of Lord Ellenborough of England, contacted us. He was a student at Trinity College in Dublin and had read about the girl's death in the newspapers.

He said he had made contact with her through a dating agency and confirmed that she arrived in Swords, where he lived, on Saturday 6 September, at around 12.30 p.m. They went back to his flat and chatted for a while before he gave her a small tour of the village. At 2.30 p.m., Mr Law said he walked Deborah Robinson to the bus stop and offered to travel to Dublin with her. She said that was not necessary and smiled and waved goodbye to him as he walked away.

Thousands of questionnaires were issued in Swords and Naas for help with the investigation. We established that Ms Robinson had boarded the bus for Dublin City and one witness, a nun, confirmed seeing her on it. But what happened to her after that? No one knew.

Dr Tim Creedon from the Forensic Laboratory now came to our assistance. It is an established fact that a man's semen group matches his blood. From an examination of the semen found on the girl, Dr Creedon established that the man had a blood group common to only 20 per cent of the male population of Ireland. The doctor made another, even more important discovery, a surprisingly high number of yarn fragments on the dead girl's jeans.

The yarns were a mix of cotton and polyester in different colours. He concluded that they were fibres from a factory that used woven and knitted fabrics to produce lightweight garments. He felt that the wide range of colours and yarns ruled out large companies dealing in bulk orders and pointed to a factory with a small work force, making up a variety of materials for small orders.

Dr Creedon also established that the yarn fragments did not originate from the textile factory where Ms Robinson had worked. There were 21 different fragments involved. We believed that they had adhered to her jeans only a short time prior to her death, as had she gone outside, they would have fallen off.

Now I had something to work on. Officers visited numerous textile factories and returned with samples of fibres for Dr Creedon to analyse. It was a painstaking and difficult operation. Factories regularly change their samples, and here we were looking for samples dating 6 months back.

Finally, after months of checking countless samples from over a dozen companies we found a match from a Dublin city factory, Janet Ltd.

Enquiries into the background of people connected with Janet Ltd led us to a former employee, Richard O'Hara, aged 28 and a native of Belfast. He had previous criminal convictions in Northern Ireland and England for assault and theft. While working for Janet Ltd, he lived in a flat in Dublin's Parnell Street, with his wife and children.

On 6 September, the day Deborah Robinson travelled to Dublin, he had been working overtime at the factory until 2 p.m. Sometime around 6.30, Patrick Flood, a director of Janet Ltd, was in a pub near the factory when O'Hara came in. He said he had been contacted by the Gardaí to close an open window in the premises. The director thought this odd. While O'Hara had a key, he was not a listed key-holder for emergencies.

On 12 September, O'Hara decided to leave his job at the factory and indicated by letter that he planned to commit suicide. He did not kill himself and subsequently returned to work and remained there until the end of September. Then he left again and went to live in Tralee, Co. Kerry. After a while, he started travelling around the country, using dud cheques. He was arrested in Co. Galway on 24 April 1981, and remanded in custody to Limerick Prison.

While there, he became mentally unstable and was transferred to the Central Mental Hospital, Dublin. A sample of his blood was taken and analysed. It confirmed that his blood grouping was the same as that identified by Dr Creedon in his semen analysis.

Following his discharge from the Central Mental Hospital, O'Hara was taken to Galway District Court in November 1981, to face the dud cheque charges against him. I had to bide my time. I could not arrest him for the murder while he was in custody awaiting trial.

Finally on 2 December 1981, the charges against him were dropped on the direction of the Director of Public Prosecutions and he was released. We immediately re-arrested him for questioning about the Deborah Robinson murder, and he agreed 'to make a full statement about the girl I killed in Dublin on a Saturday in Dublin in September 1980'.

It had happened on the first Saturday in September because, I now remember it was on the following Saturday 13 September, I went to Confession to tell the priest about it. It was all my fault.

I finished work at about 12.30 p.m. and I went home to my flat at Parnell Street, Dublin, where I was then living with my wife and three children. I had an argument with my wife, who was going shopping. I left the flat and went down to Sheriff Street to get a fix. When I got the fix, I went to the Film Centre near O'Connell Bridge. The film was about a robbery, but I was not paying attention. I was just sitting there.

I left about 5 p.m. and walked up to Roches Stores in Henry Street, where I thought I would meet my wife. I did not see my wife — if I had, I would not be in this mess. I met two girls outside Roches Stores and I knew one of them, as she worked with me in the factory in East Arran Street. She was about 15 years old and from Sheriff Street and worked one of the machines and I spoke to this girl for a few minutes.

I then went to a bar nearby and had a drink or two. When I left the bar, I walked up towards home. I met a girl walking down Parnell Street, near the Rotunda Hospital, going towards Capel Street. She spoke to me and I got into conversation with her. I walked down Parnell Street with her towards Capel Street and up by the Technical College. I told her I was married and had three children. She told me her name was Deb or Debbie.

We walked down towards the markets and I saw Patrick Flood's car parked outside a pub near the factory. He was one of my bosses. I told her to walk on and I would be with her in a minute. I went into the pub and spoke to Patrick Flood, and he asked me did I want a drink and I said no.

I went back to the girl Debbie and we walked around the block. I had the keys of the factory and we went in. We sat in the canteen talking. I switched off the alarm on the way in. She told me she worked in some weavers off Sandy Row in Belfast. She had a look around the factory and I made two joints. She would not have one. She was talking about travel and a language course.

In his statement O'Hara described how they had sexual intercourse. But this claim was hotly disputed by Deborah Robinson's family after the court case. He claimed she consented to sex, but the State Pathologist's report said she had been a victim of forced sexual intercourse, as the marks and bruising on her body proved.

'I felt bad because the love act was not right,' said O'Hara in his statement.

> I told her to put her jeans on. She pulled them off the table by the legs and I started pulling up my own trousers. She had some trouble with her zip and said something to me. I don't know what it was. I felt lousy about what she had said to me earlier. We talked and she told me she had to get a bus home. It was late, I think it was after seven. We phoned CIE and I spoke to a girl and she said Ulster Bus had nothing to do with them. She started shouting and said: 'how am I going to get home?'. She kept on shouting and was out in the hall, at the front.

> I told her to keep her voice down. I put my hand over her mouth and she said: 'don't tell me what to do'. I put my hands tight around her neck and squeezed and she seemed to flake, you know, get weak. I thought she had fainted. I fuckin' cracked when I realised she was dead. I got water and put it on a cloth to see if she would come around. I lifted her into the cutting room and left her on polythene bags. I left the factory and did not set the alarm.

> I walked down the quays and looked into the Liffey. I just walked around for a while and went home. I sat on a chair in the livingroom and my wife came down from the bed and said something to me, and went back to bed. I just sat there. I did not go to bed. She came down the next morning and made the kids their breakfast. Sunday afternoon, I went back to the factory and I knew it was all true to life, that Deb or Debbie was dead.

> I left and went away to get a vehicle. I went to Budget-Rent-A-Car off O'Connell Street. The fellow there knew me and he had nothing to hire. He said he was expecting a van back and he asked me to call back at five or half five. When I went back later, I got a white Hiace van. I drove the van down to the factory. I went into the factory and Debbie was cold and stiff. I brought her out and put her in the van.

> I drove down the Quays and followed the flow of traffic on to the Naas dual carriageway. I drove off the main road. I could not stand her in the van. I had to get her out. It was still light and I lowered her into an open ditch where there was no water.

I drove back to Dublin and left the van outside the car hire company. The place was closed. I was locking up the van when I realised her shoes, hat and other things were in it. I wrapped them up in newspaper that was in the van and went up to Summerhill and threw them in the back of the flats. I then went home.

At the Central Criminal Court in Dublin, on 29 March 1982, Richard O'Hara was found guilty of the murder of Deborah Robinson and sentenced to life imprisonment. Afterwards, the dead girl's father thanked me for bringing her killer to justice.

In the High Court in Dublin on 21 September 1996, O'Hara's appeal to be freed, after 15 years behind bars, was rejected.

17 'I'VE LOST MY FAMILY, GOD FORGIVE ME.'...

THERE WERE five coffins. One of them contained the badly burned body of 29-year-old Mary Norris. The others, small and white, held the remains of her four daughters — Catherine, aged 12, Sabrina, who was 9, 7-year-old Fiona, and the baby of the family, Deirdre, just 3.

The Dublin church was thronged with mourners, most of them in tears. It was a heart-rending scene. And the story of how all five had died, trapped in their home, which had been deliberately set ablaze, was one of unbelievable horror.

It was also a shocking story of drink, poverty and wife-battering. Above all, it was the story of James Norris, father of the family, and a violent, cruel bully. His proudest boast was that he could drink anyone under the table and a barman at his local testified that he could down 30 pints of Guinness at a sitting and still not appear drunk. His family, however, had to pay an appalling price for such excesses.

James Norris and Mary, his common law wife, were well known around Neilstown, in the Dublin suburb of Clondalkin. Norris was a heavy drinker and gambler. From their social welfare and children's allowance he would give his wife five pounds to last her the week, while he used the rest of the money to finance addiction.

For a while, they supplemented their income through crime, burgling houses on nearby estates. Mary Norris, slim and petite, was hoisted up to small windows by her husband and then unlocked front doors to let him in. They stole anything and everything of value, loading the goods into a baby's pram which they then pushed close to their local bar for a quick sale. On a good night they would get as much as £200 for the stolen property. Both had convictions for theft.

Begging was another way of raising money. Mary Norris dressed her youngest daughter, aged three, in rags and they travelled regularly to Dublin City to beg on the streets.

One day, a total stranger took pity on them and opened a bank account in Mary Norris's name in Clondalkin. He allowed her to withdraw £25 a week and he also bought her a suite of furniture. He warned her not to tell her alcoholic husband about their arrangement. The extra money was a godsend as the £5 her husband gave her every week didn't go very far on food. As the week wore on, her children walked around the housing estate and begged food from the neighbours.

Mary Norris was so small and slim that she was able to wear her eldest daughter Catherine's clothes. Her favourite outfit was the child's confirmation suit, which she wore the night before she died. The Social Services looked after the family as best they could. They had electricity — some of their neighbours did not — a cooker and a TV.

Like her husband — or more probably, because of him — Mary Norris drank a lot. She also took valium and sleeping tablets. When drunk and cold, she threw what clothes were nearest to hand on the fire in an attempt to keep warm. If her supply of teabags ran out, she sent her 3-year-old daughter across the road, in her nightdress, to collect some from a friend, often as late as midnight.

Her husband never had a good word for anyone, according to those who knew him. When he was not drinking, he expected the best of food at home. Once, when his wife brought him back the wrong type of fish for his supper, a witness saw him punch her in the face. She did not react. When he was seen punching her again in the local public house, a woman intervened to warn that his wife's skull could not take that kind of punishment for long. 'Let's see what your skull can take,' said Norris, hitting her a vicious blow on the forehead and knocking her unconscious. On another occasion, during a card game outside the pub, one of the players annoyed Norris and they argued. When the man threatened to fight, Norris pulled down his trousers and began to defecate on the footpath. The man walked away in disgust. Norris, however, did not forget the incident. Later, armed with a heavy stick, he waited for the other man and attacked him, without warning, outside the family home. He broke the stick across the man's neck and they fell down together in a desperate struggle. As Norris began to get the worst of things, he shouted for his son, Jason. Eleven-year-old Jason came running and his father ordered him to go to the kitchen and get a knife. The child returned with the knife to the scene of the fight, which was still going on. 'Stab him, Jason,' shouted his father. 'No, da, I cannot,' answered the disturbed child. 'Stab him now or I'll break your neck,' screamed his father. Jason stabbed the man, though without much force, in the chest and buttocks, causing him minor injuries. After that, Norris took to carrying a screwdriver, in case his victim sought revenge.

Norris used ferrets for hunting. A friend, providing evidence that he could be as cruel to animals as to people, told how he had called to show him a new white ferret he had acquired. To amuse those present, he shoved the animal down his trousers. The trick went horribly wrong as the ferret bit him repeatedly on his testicles. Norris ran screaming from the house. Later, when the friend called to see if he had recovered, he noticed an unusual smell. Norris told him he had burnt the ferret alive and then fed it to his dogs in the back yard.

On the 7 July 1987, Norris demanded half the children's allowance which his wife had collected that morning and set off for the pub where he drank nine pints of Guinness. At three o'clock he went home and watched television with his children until nine o'clock. Then he demanded the remainder of the children's allowance, £20, and went back to the bar.

Later his wife Mary joined him. He drank nine pints of Furstenburg while his wife had four pints of Guinness. They arrived home after midnight and watched TV with Jason and Catherine until 1 a.m. when they all went to bed. During the night the house went on fire and Mary Norris and her four daughters died.

I was on holiday in Kerry when I heard about the tragedy. I rang Detective Sergeant Michael Carolan (now a Chief Superintendent) to find out the details. He told me that the circumstances were suspicious and so I decided to return to Dublin to take charge of the investigation. The only survivors, James Norris and son Jason, were questioned and their stories conflicted with those of the firemen and witnesses. A next door neighbour told of hearing Mary Norris shouting during the night: 'leave my kids alone' and: 'leave me alone'. Later he was awakened by Catherine Norris screaming: 'Help, help, I can't breathe'.

Another neighbour said that at 3.27 a.m., awakened by the noise of an argument, she looked out and saw James Norris standing in his front garden shouting repeatedly: 'You're all a pack of bastards'. She got the impression he was fighting with his wife and daughters. Thirteen minutes later, she saw black smoke rising from the front of the house and rang the fire brigade. She was told the fire had already been reported.

A woman living nearby said that at 3.30 a.m. she heard glass breaking and a woman screaming. She then heard a voice shout: 'get the fecking children,' and saw flames coming from the kitchen of the house, No. 1 Liscarne Gardens. She watched the house until the fire brigade arrived 15 minutes later. During that time she saw James Norris standing with his back to the end wall of his house. He stood motionless in that position for 10 minutes and made no attempt to stop the fire or to assist his family. All the time the flames were growing stronger and spreading, she said.

Eventually she saw him move at normal pace towards the front of his house. He still did not shout for help. Then she spotted another man arriving on the scene.

Christopher O'Reilly saved Jason Norris's life. On arrival at the house, at 3.40 a.m., he met James Norris, standing in the front garden shouting: 'Mary, wake up.' He said to O'Reilly: 'The kids are in there and she's in there. I can't get in'. O'Reilly tried to force the front door open, but it was locked. The rear of the ground floor was now engulfed in flames and there was smoke coming from the large front bedroom.

He kept banging on the front door until he succeeded in waking young Jason who was sleeping in the box room above the front door. Jason, still half asleep, opened his window and jumped down into the man's arms.

A taxi driver who was passing stopped to see if he could help. He recalled seeing James Norris and thought that he was not too interested or sad over what was happening. That view was supported by another passerby, who said Norris told her that his wife and children were still inside the house, but 'they are probably all gone now'. He then asked the woman for a cigarette.

Mary Norris and her four daughters had all died from carbon monoxide poisoning and extensive burns. Jason and James Norris were taken by ambulance to hospital for checks, but were relatively unscathed.

Nine days after the tragedy I arrested James Norris. During

questioning, he claimed that he had been wakened by Jason, who told him the house was on fire. He had called to his wife, he said, and they both began searching for their clothes.

He told us he had opened the door of the girls' bedroom but black smoke came out and there was no sound from the children. He had told Jason to get out quickly, but then lost sight of him. His lungs were full of smoke and flames were coming up the stairs. He did not call the girls, as he felt he did not have enough time. He returned to the back bedroom, but did not see his wife there, and then got out through the window of that bedroom and dropped to the ground. He claimed that he could not have done any more for his family as he was suffering from smoke inhalation.

I knew that Norris was lying in his statement. We could prove that Jason's bedroom had not been opened while the fire was in progress, as there was no evidence of fire damage or smoke stains on the inside of the door or doorframe. We established that Mary Norris had not left her bedroom. Her remains were removed from there by a fireman. The most damning evidence of all was the discovery by a fireman that the window of James and Mary Norris's bedroom was locked on the inside. It was opened later to ventilate the smoke-filled building. We interrogated Norris for hours. Finally, when he realised that we did not believe him, he made another statement, in which he first revealed some of his previous experiences with arson.

He admitted burning two houses previously occupied by him in Coolock and Ballyfermot so as to obtain a transfer. In each case he wanted a transfer because he did not get on with his neighbours, or he didn't like the area. Detectives checked these claims and found they were true. He then told us he would reveal what really occurred on the night of the fire.

> After we went to bed, I told Mary that I was afraid that (the neighbour he beat with the stick) would gain revenge and Mary told me, 'don't mind him, it will blow over'. I would not accept what she said and our voices were raised about this. Mary was asleep before I got up, pulled on my trousers and went downstairs.
>
> I went into the kitchen and sat on the couch. I was afraid of him (his neighbour) and after sitting on couch for at least an hour, I decided that I would burn the house to damage the kitchen, so that I would get rehoused in another area of Clondalkin altogether. I set fire to the couch, which was a brown leather one. The leather was cut in the arm with foam hanging out.

The couch blazed up immediately and hit the ceiling. I did not stay around to see where the blaze spread to. I was running up the stairs and I looked back behind me to find the flames and smoke coming up after me. I went into a panic and did not know what to do at the time because I did not think it would spread that fast.

I was nearly at the top of the stairs at this time and I turned around and jumped from the top of the stairs to the hallway. I just about succeeded in getting out the front door. It was then that I burnt my feet and elbow.

The front door closed after me. I started to scream for Mary to get out of the back of the house and I went around to the front and started to shout again, calling Catherine, my daughter, and the other girls to get up. Most of the smoke was coming from the windows at the back of the house.

The caretaker from the old people's flats told me that he had sent for the fire brigade. I was shouting, for feck's sake, will you get out quick. I was shouting this to get my wife and children out. I remember Christy O'Reilly taking Jason, my son, out. At one stage, before the ambulance and fire brigade arrived, I ran across the road to the railings and knelt down and held on to the railing, saying: 'Oh God, no no no'.

'I heard a person saying, 'that's Mr Norris.' It was two gardaí and they lifted me up and brought me to an ambulance and that's where I saw Jason next. The gardaí put me sitting beside Jason in the ambulance. The two of us were crying together in the ambulance and while we were there, a fireman came along. He was carrying something in his arms. I did not know what it was at first that he was carrying and then I saw that it was Deirdre, my baby. I knew that she was dead and I just leapt from the ambulance shouting: 'No, No, No, God, oh no'. Somebody came along behind me and I was taken to St Vincent's Hospital where I was treated for the burns to my arm and feet.

When I started the fire, I did not mean to harm them. I just wanted a change of house like before, when nobody got hurt. I had a lot of drink taken that day and night. I was not used to drinking the Furstenburg lager and I found it very strong.

I am totally shattered by the fire as I lost my wife and four lovely daughters, God forgive me. I wish I could put the clock back. I will never be able to hold my head up again.

Later Norris added: 'The reason I did not tell the truth earlier was that I was afraid of what might happen to me.' He said he was scared of what his wife's family might do to him.

He also told us:

> I remember a while back, I hit Mary, my wife, with a red hot poker. There were a number of other occasions when I hit her with my fists. I don't know the reason I used to hit her so often. It was my own bad temper, I suppose. I always had a bad temper and it gets worse when I have drink taken.
>
> I was in a bad temper the night I burned the house at Liscarne Gardens. I'm lucky that Shane, who was staying with a friend, and Jason are still alive. Mary and the girls will forgive me.

He then broke down and cried for a while.

Norris, by his own admission, was very experienced in burning houses. On the two previous occasions he took the precaution of evacuating his family before the fire and had even removed valuable items of property from one house before setting it ablaze. On this occasion, however, he took no such precautions. I concluded that in the course of a quarrel with his wife, he maliciously set fire to the house with the intention of killing her and his family.

On 18 July, he was charged with his wife's murder. As he was being driven away past the blackened shell of his former home, he cowered on the floor of the patrol car, behind the rear seat and wailed. At the subsequent trial in the Central Criminal Court in 1988, he was found guilty and sentenced to penal servitude for life. At the time of writing, he is still in custody.

18 DANCE OF DEATH: MY LAST CASE...

TWO YOUNG girls out walking in Glencullen, Co. Dublin, found the body. The victim was Patricia Furlong, slender, fair-haired, and just 21. She had been strangled with her own clothing and her body dumped in a field close to the centre of the village festival.

The case, which was to be my last as head of the Murder Squad, earned a place in the record books. The body was discovered on July 24 1982, but it was not until nine years later that my principal suspect, Vincent Connell, former prison officer, radio disc jockey and ladies' man, stood in the dock.

His trial cost £1m and lasted 42 days, the longest murder trial in the State's history. After an absence of almost seven hours, the jury returned a verdict of guilty and he was sentenced to life imprisonment.

By then I had cleared my desk and retired from the Force, but the case had not ended. Four years later, the Court of Criminal Appeal quashed the murder conviction and Connell, while subsequently pleading guilty to a number of lesser charges, walked free.

The investigating team established that Patricia Furlong attended the Fraughan Festival in Glencullen on the night she was killed. Her body was found in a field about 100 yards from the dance tent. Statements were taken from hundreds of people who had attended the festival, but despite an intensive investigation, no one was arrested.

Then, two years later, in 1984, a woman who had been at the dance on the night of the murder, changed her statement. She told us that her fiancée at the time had gone missing from the dance tent for three quarters of an hour without any explanation. The man, Vincent Connell, had since emigrated, first to England, then to South Africa. Five years later he returned home, and became the focus of the investigation. Checking on his background, I learned that in 1978 Gillian Kane, a Dubliner, met him when he was a prison officer in Mountjoy and a disc jockey with Big D Radio. They got engaged that Christmas, but their relationship began to deteriorate shortly afterwards.

> Two days after the engagement, Vincent and I went to Kelly's Hotel at George's Street. Vincent had been drinking all that day. At approx. 1 a.m. 27.12.78 I decided to go home. We had an argument over this and I ordered a taxi and I told Vincent to stay as long as he liked. I went to the Ladies Toilet. Vincent followed me and punched me viciously on the head and face. The next thing I remember was waking up in a bed in the hotel the following morning. There was blood all over the sheet and pillowcase. Vincent was holding my hand and saying he was sorry for what he did. The right side of my face was cut, bruised and swollen. It took two months for the bruising and swelling to go down.

In February 1980, she broke off the engagement despite protests from Connell and pleas that she reconsider. Ms Kane emigrated to England for three years and returned to Dublin in 1986. She heard that Vincent Connell had emigrated to South Africa and had married there.

After Ms Kane broke off their engagement, Vincent Connell began dating Mary Creedon, another Dubliner. They got engaged in April, 1982. On Friday 23 July of that year, she attended the Fraughan Festival in Glencullen with him. They drank in Johnny Fox's pub in Glencullen before moving to the beer tent which was part of the festival. She noticed a girl near the entrance to the tent, talking to some people. Connell said he knew her and went over to talk to her. When he returned to the tent some 45 minutes later, he was in a bad humour and on the way home asked his fiancée to go away with him the following morning.

The next day Ms Creedon told Connell that a woman had been murdered at the festival the previous night and that the Gardaí at Stepaside were anxious to interview everyone who attended festival. He agreed to go with her. She told the Gardaí that he had only left the tent to go to the toilet, and did not mention his 45-minute absence.

Nearly two years later, on 12 March 1984, Ms Creedon changed her statement to the police. By October 1982, her relationship with Vincent Connell had ended. She had left him, worried by his irrational behaviour. She said she had not told the truth at the original interview because Vincent Connell had been watching her closely and she felt intimidated.

Connell had been born in London in 1951, an only child of Irish parents. His father was from Carlow and his mother from Kilkenny, and they had separated when he was 19. He moved to Dublin with his mother and lived with her and an aunt in a house in Terenure. Considered generally as a likeable, capable sort, he had no problems settling in the city. By the end of 1982 he had moved to Liverpool and shortly afterwards went to South Africa.

In January 1990, Detective Wall of Dublin's Sundrive Road Garda Station was telephoned by Vincent Connell, who asked to meet him. He claimed he was being blackmailed over an assault he allegedly committed on Barbara Rooney, an ex-girlfriend, and asked Garda Wall to help. The detective realised that this was the same Vincent Connell wanted for questioning with regard to incidents concerning Gillian Kane. He told his superior, Detective Sergeant Gerry O'Carroll.

I believed that Connell was trying to discover from talking to the detective if the Gardaí had connected him to the killing of Patricia Furlong. On 19 May 1990, I sent a team to search his house in Terenure. My worry now was that his aunt would tell him about the search and he would flee from the country so I instructed Detective Wall to contact the aunt and to pretend that he had just been looking for Connell in connection with the blackmailing claim.

That day Connell was attending a party in Ashbourne, County Meath at the home of a middle-aged woman he had met through a dating agency. The woman, named Anne, recalled how his mood changed after he telephoned his aunt and talked to her. He also telephoned Detective Wall and arranged to meet him the next day.

According to his host, he seemed to lose concentration and was unable to finish the barbecue he was preparing after the call to his aunt. He kept repeating that 'the whole thing is bothering me'. Then he got drunk and fell asleep on a couch but when some of the guests tried to lift him, he fell on to the tiled floor. As they tried to move him him upstairs to a bedroom, he fell down the stairs and tried to make it to the door to go home. He became aggressive and one of the guests refused to go near him. Two women guests coaxed him halfway up the stairs until he collapsed in through the toilet door and fell to the floor. They left him there. He had drunk three quarters of a bottle of brandy and a half bottle of whiskey. The party-goers retired to bed at 4.30 a.m. leaving Connell — who had dressed up as a priest to entertain them — on the floor in the toilet. On the Sunday Anne had returned from Mass to find him gone.

When Connell turned up to meet Detective Wall in The Fleet bar in Dublin that Sunday, we arrested him. During the car trip to Tallaght Garda Station he had to be physically restrained. He shouted to passersby that he was being kidnapped.

While he was the No. 1 suspect for the murder of Patricia Furlong, I instructed the interrogation team to limit their queries to other incidents. Vincent Connell would admit nothing and a tense dogged battle of words began. The following day Gillian Kane came to the interview room, hopeful of producing a reaction and we subjected him to an intense verbal examination in her presence. He did not confess to anything. I sensed, though, a wavering of his steely resolve. My men shifted their line of enquiry to the murder case, and Vincent Connell stumbled and fell into our trap.

It was put to Vincent Connell that he had left the beer tent at the Faughan Festival for three quarters of an hour. He replied that his former girlfriend, Mary Creedon, was lying. The investigator told him that Ms Creedon was willing, like Gillian Kane, to come to the interview room and repeat what she said in front of him. By the time she arrived at the station, he had cracked. Suddenly, he said: 'Look, I met Trish'. Asked why he had been reluctant to admit he left the beer tent that night for three quarters of an hour, he paused and stared into space for five minutes before replying: 'I did something terrible that night.' He was cautioned and then added: 'I went mad and killed her'. On two aerial photographs, he marked where he had left Patricia Furlong's body, her handbag and other items, which he had thrown away.

In a statement he told of going to the Festival with Ms Creedon, and said the main reason was to meet RTE's Robert Gahan. 'We met Mr Gahan and I discussed the possibility of getting into RTE.' After that they went to the beer tent where 'there were some people I knew from the local Fianna Fáil Cumann'.

Later he met Trish and spent some time talking to her.

> We were talking about roller-skating, probably, because she was a customer of mine at the Top Hat in Dun Laoghaire, where I was assistant manager. She had aspirations to get on to my roller disco dancing team. When she used to come to the Top Hat, she always came to me and acknowledged me. She did not come to me for roller skating lessons.
>
> After a few minutes, she and I decided to go for walk down the road. Somewhere down the road we saw a gate. It was locked, but we climbed over it. She was very tipsy, so I had to help her over it. I put my arm around her shoulder and she then slapped me across the face. We were a good few yards into the field when this happened. This really incensed me and I hit her back.
>
> Then I lost my rag altogether and began to choke her with my hands. She began to scream and I had to stop her. She fell to the ground. Then, during the struggle, the clothing from the top half of her body came up around her neck. At this stage she had stopped shouting. The clothes that came up around her neck were a T-shirt, bra and some type of light jacket. I pulled this clothing up around her mouth and neck to stop her from shouting. I panicked and tied them around her neck and squeezed them.
>
> Actually there was very little struggle. Her handbag fell to the ground and some of its contents fell out. There was a little make-up, door keys, perfume and a little diary. I can't recall any money. There were some women's toiletries. I took the diary and some of the cosmetics away with me and then threw them into a ditch at the back of Johnny Fox's pub on my way back to the beer tent. I threw the bag down the field from where Trish was lying.
>
> I then went back to the beer tent to Mary. There was a kind of fight going on. I don't know what I said to Mary when I went back. I was very upset, but I did not tell Mary what happened. We stayed on in the beer tent for a short time after that and went home at about 3 a.m. I heard the next day that she died. I did not know that she was dead when I left, as she was breathing lightly. When I met Trish I had no intention of killing her. I did not mean to do it.

The suspect appeared to be happier after making the confession. He even sang a song. Later on, in court, he denied everything and claimed we coerced him into making the statement. As he was escorted to

Mountjoy, he told the officer in charge that he feared for his safety as he had once been a warden in the prison. He was assured that he would be safe. Then he remarked: 'I should not have made the statement.'

At the trial Connell complained that he had not slept for 48 hours while in detention in Tallaght Garda Station. We proved that he was left alone for sleeping periods but chose not to avail of them. He claimed violence had been used to make him sign the statement, and that we composed it ourselves. He tried to substantiate these claims by referring to marks on his body. We proved he was bruised and marked after falling while drunk at the party in Ashbourne.

In the 1,350 statements taken from people at the festival, some had said that they saw Patricia Furlong alive at 1.30 a.m. on the night of the murder. Ms Creedon's evidence was that the accused had returned to the beer tent at 1.30 a.m. So if what these witnesses said was correct, he could not have killed her. The prosecuting team responded that these young witnesses who claimed to have seen Ms Furlong alive were mostly drunk at the time and could not be certain of when they last saw her.

A scientific method of analysis was used by the defence team to try to prove that the confession was written by the Gardaí. Examples of the accused's speech patterns and mode of expression were compared with the statement in an effort to discredit it. The jury were not convinced. On 19 December 1991, after deliberating for six and a half hours they returned a unanimous verdict of guilty.

Vincent Connell, sitting close by his barrister, Blaise O'Carroll, was shocked. He stood up and faced the judge, who was preparing to deliver the sentence, and in a quivering voice declared: 'My Lord I am not guilty. I did not kill that woman.' As Judge Richard Johnson sentenced him to life for the murder, Connell leaned against the bench for support and whispered: 'Oh my God, I did not kill her.'

Outside the Four Courts, the detectives celebrated with Patricia Furlong's family. Patricia's sister embraced a garda and whispered: 'Thank you'. In January 1992 the following letter was circulated by the office of the Deputy Commissioner:

> I am directed by the Commissioner to inform you that on 10 January 1992, three members of the deceased family called to his office to express their appreciation and thanks to the Gardaí for the manner in which they conducted the investigations into their sister's murder.

They also wanted to put on record their admiration for the manner in which the members withstood the very caustic and demeaning cross-examination during the trial.

The death of their sister in such horrific circumstances was most difficult to come to terms with and they had to relive it all during the trial. Without the sympathy and understanding shown by the Gardaí they would have found it very difficult to cope. They asked that their gratitude be brought to the notice of all the gardaí involved.

In April 1995, the Court of Criminal Appeal quashed the murder conviction against Vinnie Connell on the grounds that he had been denied his constitutional right to see his solicitor while in custody.

At a subsequent trial he pleaded guilty to charges of assault against four former girlfriends in the 1970s and 1980s — Gillian Kane (1978), Agnes Long (1981), Mary Creedon (1981) and Barbara Rooney (1989).

19 'THE HEAVY GANG'

IN 1991 I retired from the Force after 43 years' service. During those years I had witnessed many changes, but the biggest was unquestionably the growth in crime, particularly following the outbreak of the Troubles in Northern Ireland after 1969.

At the time, I was based in Clondalkin, which was a difficult posting. I got great personal satisfaction from solving a number of crimes and also from trying to prevent others. There were a few major factories in the area and in my spare time I used to try to get jobs for young men from the locality so as to steer them away from a life on the wrong side of the law.

My initiative paid off in other ways. One young lad that I had helped get a job in the Volkswagen assembly plant on the Naas Road later tipped me off that large numbers of tyres were being stolen from the assembly line. The thief was taking advantage of the fact that there was very infrequent stock-taking at the plant because it was just too busy.

Through my investigation I learned that the man I was looking for was a well-known soccer player. First, of course, I had to catch him. For a time, he succeeded in getting the tyres out of the plant unnoticed, but eventually I set a trap, with the co-operation of my long-time colleagues, Thomas McIntyre and Michael Carolan who was a footballer with Kildare.

We slipped into the plant, hidden in the back of the manager's car. I hid in the rear seat and Detective Garda McIntyre was in the boot, as we did not want the regular security staff to see us. After a few hours, our suspect appeared and began moving through the tyre boxes.

Eventually, when he spotted us, he ran from the factory — and straight into the arms of Garda Carolan who was waiting outside. After a scuffle we arrested him. He admitted having taken the tyres and was later convicted. The plant management was delighted with the outcome, and so was I. Cracking a case, however small, offers a degree of personal satisfaction that makes the job worthwhile.

I also remember another early case in which a former garda was badly beaten up and robbed. He was taken to the Meath Hospital where I interviewed him briefly as he was lay dying. He told me he had been attacked by two youths dressed in football jerseys. I discovered that two youths had escaped a few days previously from Daingean Reformatory and that there had been break-ins between there and Dublin. I kept pursuing them and two years later traced them to Manchester.

My two colleagues, Michael Carolan and Tom McIntyre, travelled with me to Holyhead and we accompanied them on the boat back to Dun Laoghaire. It was an August weekend and the ferry was packed. While taking a stroll on the deck, I noticed another man who had jumped bail three years previously in connection with another crime in Clondalkin. I smiled to myself as I thought 'we'll get three prisoners from this boat for the price of two!'. As you cannot handcuff anybody on a ferry for safety reasons, we waited until we reached Dun Laoghaire. As the wanted man was walking down the gang-plank, we arrested him. All three were subsequently convicted and sent to Mountjoy.

After a period in Clondalkin, I was asked to join the Murder Squad by Chief Superintendent Patrick McLaughlin, who later became a Commissioner. In the Squad I joined another future Commissioner, Patrick Culligan, together with Chief Superintendents Dan Murphy and John Moore, both now dead. Later we were joined by the now Deputy Commissioner, John Paul McMahon, and others, including Detective Inspectors Michael Canavan and Tom Dunne, along with Detective Sergeant Christy Godkins, Chief Superintendent Tony Hickey, Superintendent P.J. Browne, Chief Superintendent Pat Culhane Superintendent Hubert Reynolds, Detective Sergeant Pat Lynagh, Detective Sergeant Tom Dunne and Detective Sergeant Gerry O'Carroll and many more.

Kidnapping was a crime of which I had no experience, a factor which weighed on my mind when Commissioner Garvey sent me to Limerick to take charge of the Herrema case. I remember being interviewed by a Dutch television crew in Limerick, who suggested that we would never solve the kidnapping because we had no experience of how to deal with it. I bluntly told them that I was certain we would free Dr Herrema and return him safely to his family.

It was a very difficult investigation. I remember being awakened one night by a phone call from the present present Commissioner, Pat Byrne, who told me that he and Detective Inspector Myles Hawkshaw were holding a suspect named Brian McGowan in Portlaoise who might provide some useful information. I drove through the night from Limerick where I was staying, and interviewed McGowan. He eventually provided the information that led to a house in Monasterevin and a breakthrough in the case.

The Herrema kidnapping certainly ranks among the most difficult crimes we had to tackle. But the patience and skill with which the marathon siege was handled, with Dr Herrema finally being rescued unharmed, won widespread praise at home and abroad.

In investigating suspected murder cases over the years, I met all types of people — normal, abnormal, odd and eccentric. During my years in the Gardaí I met people from all walks of human life. Some of the cases were not without a sense of humour, even though it did not appear so at the time. Take, for instance, the investigation into the death of Mary-Jo Kelly of Liskiltagh, Ballyourigan, Croom Co. Limerick, in April 1969.

Mary-Jo Kelly was a recluse from the world and had lived all her life with her brother John on a farm near the village of Croom. She rarely went out and was only occasionally seen by neighbours walking through the fields on the farm. Mary-Jo was aged around 50 and her brother was some 10 years older.

On 14 April 1969, the local postman reported to Sergeant O'Dea of Croom that he had not seen Mary-Jo Kelly for many months and he was concerned. Sergeant O'Dea visited John Kelly who told him that his sister had gone to Boston some time previously. When Sergeant O'Dea replied that this was impossible because his sister would have had to apply to him for a passport, Kelly still insisted that his sister was in Boston.

Eventually after further questioning, John Kelly admitted that his sister had, in fact, died and that he had buried her himself in the local cemetery without informing anybody. Sergeant O'Dea accompanied Kelly to Annahid cemetery where he pointed to a grave in which he claimed Mary-Jo was buried.

By this time, Sergeant O'Dea had become suspicious and informed Garda Headquarters in the Phoenix Park. I headed south for Croom, accompanied by Paddy Culligan (now retired Commissioner) and John McMahon (now retired Deputy Commissioner).

Having checked out the facts of the case, I obtained an Exhumation Order to open the grave in Annahid Cemetery, but to our surprise there was no recent internment. I became more suspicious of the circumstances surrounding the death of Mary-Jo Kelly and I arranged for questionnaires to be sent out locally.

The replies turned in some amazing findings. One lady, who owned a shop in Croom, said that Mary-Jo Kelly had last visited her five years previously. Another woman reported that her husband had cut her hair in July 1967. Others reported infrequent sightings of the missing woman in the fields around the house, the last of which was in June of 1968. This was April 1969.

Farming neighbours reported that John Kelly had a tendency to 'neighbourly trespass' and had stolen hay from them on occasions.

I have often noticed that people's imaginations respond to the gossip they hear about a murder case. Locals reported seeing a horse and cart tied outside Annahid Cemetery for four or five hours in August of the previous year. The local vet even reported seeing John Kelly drive his horse and cart through Croom village with a large timber box on board. I redoubled my efforts and again questioned John Kelly. Kelly's house was known locally as 'the house that Jack built' because John Kelly had built it himself. It was in an appalling state. There was no furniture of any kind and the only bed had no matress. Any items which were brought in, such as old newspapers, were forever prisoners in the house and piles of old rubbish had built up over the years. It appeared that nothing was ever thrown out.

The front yard, however, was in stark contrast. It was kept spotless, to such an extent that if a garda stamped out a cigarette, John Kelly would immediately request that the offending butt be picked up and discarded somewhere else.

Kelly was very unco-operative but I had him accompany us to Annahid Cemetery again, to the spot where he insisted that his sister

126

was buried. I asked him to say a few prayers for his dead sister. Kelly immediately went to a corner of the cemetery which was no longer in use for burials and said three Hail Marys. I told him to get up off the ground at once as there was no one buried where he was kneeling. As usual, he insisted there was. A number of weeks passed with little progress made.

One evening I returned to the farm where I questioned John Kelly at length again. Finally he admitted that his sister has died at home in May 1968. He had left the body in the house for three days, going about his daily routine as normal. Kelly said he then made a coffin out of pieces of timber, kissed his sister goodbye, placed her body inside and took the home-made coffin by horse and cart to Annahid Cemetery where he buried it. I was still suspicious but was getting nowhere. We held a meeting of senior Garda officers and decided it was time to dig up the Kelly farm.

I went again to John Kelly and told him that because of his refusal to tell the truth, we were going to dig up his farm until we found the body of his sister.

'You can go and dig up every field but you will not find her,' he said defiantly.

I decided that if Kelly had buried his sister in a field he had probably done so close by a ditch. It was unlikely that he'd dig a grave in the middle of a field. I got Garda reinforcements and, armed with probes we set about testing the ground for signs of burial. We probed the ground relatively deeply and then tested the probe for signs of rotting flesh. It was a difficult and tasteless task but it had to be done.

We started with the fields near the house and moved outwards. There was a large force of gardaí involved and no facilities, so I was lucky to be able to call on the services of an old schoolfriend, Lieutenent Larry O'Connor, then stationed at Sarsfield Barracks in Limerick. He kindly lent us a field kit to provide nourishment. The Gardaí didn't have, and as far as I am aware still don't have, any facilities of this kind for major searches.

After probing for some time, we eventually arrived at a triangular field on 9 May 1969. There, in a corner, the local Superintendent, Dick Coady, got the smell of rotting flesh from his probe. We held another meeting to decide how to dig the ground without damaging the body and any evidence of foul play. We proceeded with great caution. Having excavated a few feet of earth, we came upon empty bags which had been used for farm-meal supplies. We proceeded with even more caution. Sure enough, underneath the bags was a body, partially decomposed, but still identifiable, that had been buried in the ground without any coffin.

I sent for the Assistant State Pathologist, Dr Raymond O'Neill, who was the most competent pathologist I've met, to carry out a post-mortem on a make-shift table on the site. He confirmed that the body was that of a female who had been buried at least nine months previously. The woman had died of natural causes.

All of the time during our search, John Kelly had not come near us but continued to work on his farm as normal. I brought him to the site where we had exhumed the body.

'Now John,' I said, 'what do you make of this?'

'Ah, sure they're the bodies of two calves that died on me last spring. Don't remind me of them, I lost a fortune,' he replied.

There was no talking to this eccentric farmer.

With the post-mortem complete, Mary-Jo Kelly was given a proper burial in Annahid Cemetery in the grave which we had first dug up during our search.

We were quite satisfied that Mary-Jo Kelly had died of natural causes. While John Kelly should have reported the death to the Gardaí and the coroner, and was also in breach of the Public Heath Act for burying a body in his field, we did not press charges.

Later I heard that Kelly's mother had died some years previously and the undertaker had charged £40 for the coffin. John Kelly had commented at the time that there was no need for a coffin and that the body could just as well have been buried in the back garden.

I think that this would have to have been the most unusual case I dealt with and one I often recall.

Of the cases in which I was involved, one that generated much publicity was the so-called Kerry Babies case of 1985. What proved to be a most complex case had begun with the discovery of a dead baby on the beach in Caherciveen in South Kerry. Later a young woman from Abbeydorney in North Kerry, Joanne Hayes, was charged with the murder. The charges against Joanne Hayes and members of her family were subsequently struck out and a Tribunal of Enquiry, which lasted 82 days and was presided over by a High Court judge, Mr Justice Kevin Lynch, was established to examine all aspects of the case.

I do not propose to go into any detail on the investigation, but I would like to make the following points. I viewed this, not as a murder, but as a concealment of birth case and was merely following legal procedure in the charges I preferred. In such cases a mother may have become temporarily unstable following the birth of a child, and the courts normally take a lenient view.

There was nothing unusual in the fact that I had all the members of the Hayes family interviewed together. That has always been my practice to prevent family members forming alibis for one another.

The crucial thing for me was a statement which two detectives showed me, having interviewed Mrs Mary Hayes, the mother of Joanne. In it she outlined everything that had happened in the house on the night the child was born. I made up my mind on the basis of that statement. I knew Mrs Hayes would not condemn her daughter Joanne, nor make up a serious story like that. I also had Joanne Hayes' own statement. That was why I decided to charge her and other members of her family.

But I have never lost a night's sleep over the case because I did not set out to do any injustice to Joanne Hayes or anyone else. Why should I pick on that family above anyone else? Some people appeared to believe that the Gardaí wanted to charge the Hayes family, but that is totally wrong.

What gave rise to a lot of the publicity was the fact that the then Minister for Justice, Michael Noonan, took it on himself to set up a Tribunal of Enquiry. During the course of that Tribunal, Nurse Bridie Fuller, an aunt of Joanne Hayes, gave evidence of two babies being born in the house on the night in question. I thought that would have brought the inquiry to a swift conclusion, but it dragged on for weeks. If I and the Murder Squad had not been involved, the media would have shown little interest. The irony was that I had been on holiday at the time and had only gone to Cahirciveen because a number of gardaí involved in the investigation had asked me to help.

Some of the things subsequently printed in a book on the case, *My Own Story*, left it open to me to take legal action, but I didn't because I am not that type of person. Several times I have been wronged in the media but have never taken action, preferring to get on with my job.

Then there were the allegations about 'The Heavy Gang'! The tag came about in a very simple way. In the course of a trial following the murder of Larry White in Cork city, Paddy McEntee, S.C., arguing for the defence, referred to the 'heavy gang' coming down from Dublin. The media immediately latched on to the label and it went from there. There were reports about this 'heavy gang' going around the country beating up prisoners and innocent people. The reality was that no one, from the Commissioner down, would stand for that, and these allegations were scurrillous.

One of the things I learned from my work over the years is that while the public read the newspapers and listen to the news, they make up their own minds at the end of the day about any particular issue. Time and again, people came up to me to say they were fully supportive of our work, and that was very re-assuring, both for myself and my colleagues.

I never really worried too much about adverse publicity because I was satisfied in my own mind that we were doing our best. Frequently, however, I was very disappointed with the lack of appreciation I received in various quarters, including some of the Garda Commissioners — one in particular, who gave us little or no assistance.

When Dr Garret FitzGerald was Minister for Foreign Affairs in the mid 1970s, a number of gardaí complained to him that a so-called 'heavy gang' was in existence. That annoyed me greatly because neither the Commissioner of the time, Ned Garvey, nor myself were aware of such a 'gang'. It was a very serious allegation for members of the Force to make.

In his autobiography, *All In a Life*, he refers to this at some length. He wrote that he was 'distressed' by these reports and decided to raise the matter with the Government, and, if necessary, to threaten resignation. But he added that he changed his view because it 'would be sending conflicting signals to the public' when at the same time, the Government was introducing tougher legislation to deal with the outbreak of violence.

Dr FitzGerald admitted that the Minister for Justice, Pat Cooney, was 'unsympathetic' to the allegations, and in my view, rightly so. Dr FitzGerald claims he wrote a letter to the Taoiseach, Liam Cosgrave, outlining his concern, but the 1977 General Election intervened. In any event, Liam Cosgrave never met the gardaí concerned, nor should he have. Those officers should not have gone over the Commissioner's head. Dr FitzGerald should have first asked them if the visit had been approved by the Commissioner or by their Chief Superintendent. I believe he should have just ignored them altogether. I remember this incident was reported by Gulliver in the *Sunday Press* at the time.

Despite all this, I was later asked by Commissioner Patrick McLaughlin to investigate a complaint by Dr FitzGerald's wife, Joan, that a man had called to their door and appeared to be carrying a gun. I called to their home where I spoke to them both about the incident, and it was clear from their expression that they were surprised to see me.

I duly got on with the investigation and located the individual, who was a native of Tipperary, down on his luck, who happened to be living in the locality. He was of no danger to the FitzGeralds.

It was our job to do our best to protect the lives of citizens in the North as well as in the Republic. For instance, around that time I was asked to investigate the theft of gelignite at Tynagh Mines in Co. Galway. It was my first time down a mine and I was alarmed to discover how freely the highly dangerous explosive was left lying around the mining area without proper security. Several boxes were open and lying near the blasting area. Having investigated the whole system a man was arrested, charged and sentenced to 15 years in jail.

I discovered that the gelignite was being stolen from the mine and sent to Belfast. I was very glad to have intercepted that trail — in doing so the Murder Squad saved many lives and much property in the North. This episode showed that we were totally impartial in the performance of our duty and just got on with the job of combating serious crimes of all kinds.

As head of the murder Squad, I also had numerous dealings with members of the RUC over the years. On occasions, I found there was a reluctance to give out information about loyalist suspects. But there was help too. I remember, prior to the Pope's visit in 1979, we were concerned that there might be an assassination attempt on him by loyalist paramilitaries.

I had a very good contact in the RUC who, in turn, had strong contacts with the UDA and UVF. He was able to assure me that, despite the rumours, there would be no attack on the Pope. Consequently, I was able to go to the Commissioner, Paddy McLaughlin, and assure him that other than some maverick we knew nothing about, the Pope had nothing to fear from loyalist militants.

However, all my experiences with the RUC were not as reassuring. In 1972, for instance, I was in Buncrana in Donegal investigating the shooting of a young boy and girl. I had a suspect for the killing, a man named Taylor, a UDA member from Derry, but the RUC Detective Chief Inspector concerned kept telling me he could not locate him.

Eventually, I got in touch with another inspector I knew and he had the suspect in custody for me to interview within half an hour. The man immediately confessed to the murder.

I also had many dealings with the British police force and I did a number of courses at Wakefield Police College in Yorkshire and at Scotland Yard. I learned something from them, but I didn't feel the police there were any better at detecting crime than the Gardaí at home. In fact, I don't think they would have matched our record. Overall, I always found the British force very helpful in any investigation in which we sought their co-operation.

The Murder Squad was eventually scaled down with most of its members being reassigned. It was felt that the members of the Murder Squad were doing the job that should be done by local superintendents around the country. There was a belief that the local Gardaí should investigate the crimes in their area. We always consulted the local Gardaí, and we had the benefit of having an alternative perspective.

The remnants of the Squad are still there, but most have now retired from the Force. My view is that more than ever we need an initiative to tackle the new and different types of serious crime we have today.

The remaining members should be used to train younger members to carry on their work. This would ensure continued leadership and experience as well as the energy and enthusiasm of fresh recruits. You cannot expect local Gardaí to conduct an investigation in the same professional manner as the Murder Squad. They simply don't have the wealth of experience. Nor can they be expected to have the same focus as a team. In my time, as I've said, we had a success rate of 90 per cent. The current detection rate is half that figure. The facts speak for themselves.

Nowadays, with the emergence of contract killings, all the emphasis has to be on improving investigation techniques and detection rates. The impression seems to be abroad that you can simply contract someone to shoot an individual for a few thousand pounds. The situation is serious, but fortunately not that bad. In fact, it is very difficult to get one person to shoot another simply for monetary reward no matter how tough their background. Nor do these gunmen match their ruthless public image. In the course of my career in the Gardaí, I met a number of contract killers.

One hit man, in particular, I remember had aged years before his time and suffered from pangs of conscience over what he had done. In tackling contract killing I also believe that the DPP should consider the charge of conspiracy. This would be of great assistance in charging the people who ordered the murder in the first place.

I am confident that with the Murder Squad restored, these contract killers could be rooted out of our society very quickly. It is when things look at their bleakest and the Garda frustration is at its height, that a special effort is called for, with investigations being renewed with greater vigour and determination.

In my time in charge of the Murder Squad I didn't tolerate slackers or hangers-on. Many couldn't stick the pace and disappeared off the investigation team altogether. I was very happy to get rid of them. Officers who made excuses of going on holidays, or whatever, were dropped. I wanted total commitment.

For the Force, the leadership being provided at the top is all important. I served under a number of Garda Commissioners. The two best, in my opinion, were Ned Garvey and Patrick McLaughlin, although both left their posts in unfortunate circumstances. They were pressurised into resigning.

Ned Garvey took an action against the Government over the manner in which he was forced out and was awarded compensation. In my opinion, it was a paltry amount given the work he had done. I always felt Patrick McLaughlin made a mistake in resigning. He should have remained in his post and fought the attempt to remove him through the legal system. If he had I believe he would have retained his post as Commissioner. His resignation was a great loss to all of us.

I have known the present Commissioner, Pat Byrne, for many years and worked with him on several investigations. He has a tough task ahead of him and I wish him well. But from my experience of working with him, he certainly has the capability to do a good job.

Among the enormous difficulties which Gardaí face today, perhaps the most frustrating is that of bringing cases to court. The current procedure that all serious cases must go to the office of the Director of Public Prosecutions invariably results in long delays.

We have a tendency here to follow Britain in legal matters. They have a DPP, so we had to have a DPP. I have no criticism of the office or the

DPP himself, but before we operated through the Chief State Solicitor's Office in Dublin Castle. In cases of doubt, the Chief State Solicitor's Office referred for opinion to the Attorney-General. It was a competent office and the system worked very well. Delays were minimal and it was up to us to have our papers in order for processing. Today, the announcement that 'the file is gone to the DPP', has become a bit of a joke.

Looking back over all my years in the Garda Síochana, and as head of the Murder Squad, I can say that we have had almost 100 per cent success in our investigations. Many of the methods of collecting and matching evidence that we used over the years had not been seen in Ireland before. And have I any regrets? Well, I was totally committed to my job and the only one regret I have is that I did not have more time with my wife, Mary, and my family. Had I been like some others, I would have just done a certain amount of work and ensured that I had plenty of time at home and for holidays with my family. But in my own way I felt that I — and the team who worked with me — were making a contribution to the security of the State. That gave me a great deal of satisfaction.

The final verdict on my contribution is for others to deliver. I think I did a reasonable job.